Always Returning

Always Returning

The Wisdom *of* Place

15th ANNIVERSARY EDITION

d.a. hickman

Capturing Morning Press

Published by

Capturing Morning Press

Copyright © 1999, 2014 by Daisy Ann Hickman

All rights reserved.
No part of this book as updated for this edition may be reproduced or utilized in any form or by any means, electronic or mechanical, including photocopying, recording, or by any information storage or retrieval system, without permission in writing from the publisher.

Second Edition
Print ISBN-13: 978-0-9908423-5-4
E-book ISBN-13: 978-0-9908423-7-8

Produced in the United States of America

capturingmorningpress.com

CMP@capturingmorningpress.com

"Always Returning" by D.A. Hickman, previously published in *Pasque Petals*, South Dakota State Poetry Society.

~

First Edition September 1999 hardcover Eagle Brook imprint
William Morrow and Company, Inc.
(as acquired by HarperCollins Publishers Inc.)
New York, NY

Hardcover (first edition):
Where the Heart Resides—Timeless Wisdom of the American Prairie

ISBN-10: 0-688-16884-1
ISBN-13: 978-0688168841

Library of Congress first edition LCCN: 2001274827

Book photography, first edition, by artist Bob H. Miller.
Known for dream narrative collage and large scale paintings, Miller lives in Rapid City, South Dakota.
bobhbobh@rushmore.com

This edition is dedicated to our eternal longing.

Also to these bright lights of the prairie,
only here for a time:

Anna McCormick Arch
Frances Nickel Jones
Myril John Arch
Wileta Welty Hawkins
Mary Jewel Ledbetter
A.B. "Bud" Tyler, Jr.

With special mention:
Vivian June Norris

Anna M. Arch, 1889–1987, the author's beloved grandmother

ALWAYS RETURNING

where did life begin if not
on a return trip . . . from
somewhere or something?
like faded white lilies or
autumn leaves that feed
the earth only to return with
the persistence of spring,
life is a basket of motion:
coming back, coming round.

~ D.A. Hickman, 2011

CONTENTS

Acknowledgments	ix
Preface: 15th Anniversary Edition	xiii
Introduction: Growing up Prairie Wise	1
1 A Dance with Destiny	11
2 Open Space	35
3 A Steady Beat	47
4 Habits of the Heart	57
5 Almost Anything Once	67
6 Weathering the Storm	79
7 Noticeable Vibrancy	89
8 A Sense of Poetry	101
9 In a Circle	111

10	Embrace the Past	125
11	A State of Mind	135
12	The Prairie Connection	145
13	A Certain Brilliance	155
14	Zoom Lens	167
15	Spice It Up	173
16	Borrow It, Don't Buy It	183
17	The Merits of Challenge	189
18	Generous Spirit	197
19	Tell Stories	207
20	Come and Go	221
	Epilogue	231
	References	233
	About the Author	237

ACKNOWLEDGEMENTS

A WARM THANK YOU TO Michele DeFilippo, owner, 1106 Design, "a Phoenix-based company that works with authors, publishers, business pros, coaches, consultants, speakers . . . anyone who wants a beautiful book, meticulously prepared to industry standards." Michele is ever so willing to answer a stream of questions (and I'm sure many are repetitive) so authors can make informed decisions.

Thanks also to the artistic photographers who contributed to *Always Returning:* Jael Photography (author) and Kernit Grimshaw Photography (cover).

Nothing creative is ever accomplished without the help and support of family, friends, and pets who patiently sleep near your feet as you write or remind you with eager eyes, tails wagging, to take a break. I would especially like to thank those professionals who helped me review photographs, and generous colleagues who answered questions and faithfully inspired me along the way—including all the wonderful voices shared in this edition.

Always Returning

Finally, a special note of gratitude is extended to the ingenious creator of the plains, the prairies.

The spiritual dimension of landscape—of place and people—has been a comforting companion and priceless gift in my life, one I am deeply honored to celebrate, to share. Since a girl—I was two in this photo—I've been drawn to the wonder and power of open spaces and majestic skyscapes. To the artistry of nature and the connection to a higher power such landscapes suggest.

In the end, aren't we always returning to the wisdom of place?

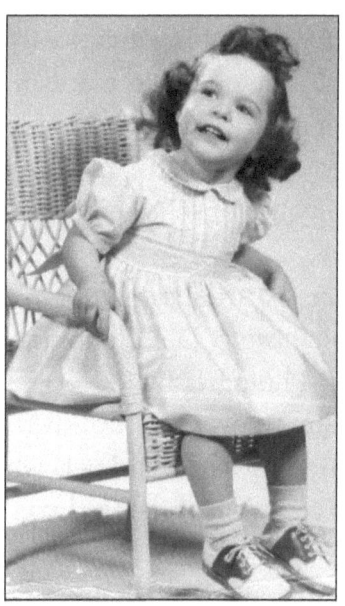

Over all, rocks, wood, and water, brooded the spirit of repose, and the silent energy of nature stirred the soul to its inmost depths.
~THOMAS COLE (1801–1848),
Essay on American Society, 1835

PREFACE

It's such an honor to release the second edition—a 15th anniversary edition—of *Where the Heart Resides: Timeless Wisdom of the American Prairie*. Given the inevitable surge of time, my book features a new title, updated content where appropriate, edited chapter titles, a new cover design, and a new dedication. It was a pleasure to work on this edition, because everything still resonated with me—perhaps, more so. The beauty of sky and land, still intoxicating, still *true*.

I wrote *Heart Resides* in 1998—published it in September, 1999—when we lived in Missouri. But, as my new title suggests, I've had the good fortune to return to my beloved prairie roots—to a place that firmly lives on in my memory, and otherwise.

The eerie dance of time, nearly invisible when gazing on a vast open space.

Returning to South Dakota in August of 2008, ten years had already elapsed since I'd carved out an accessible set of ideas and observations coined prairie wisdom. Of course my perceptions deepened during the years that interceded—as my spiritual awareness expanded—and I realized that whenever we are deeply aware of our surroundings, wisdom (inner knowing) is available to us. Thus, the new title: *Always Returning—The Wisdom of Place*.

This happens to be my place—this prairie landscape, the people who inhabit this terrain, and the lifestyle that has evolved—but you have your place, as well. Perhaps it's also in Dakota, or maybe it's in Wyoming, Pennsylvania, or Florida, or intrinsic to a wild city landscape that rings with noise: night and day. Or your place might be in a foreign country. Maybe you are homeless, or between jobs, or moving cross country. Maybe you reside in an institution, a special home for seniors or people with disabilities, or perhaps you *still* live with your parents. Wherever you find yourself, the most important thing is to be there fully. Not as a visitor, your shifting gaze drawn elsewhere, but in body and soul, as you come to know the completeness of each moment, finding wisdom in everything you see and encounter.

Poet Mary Oliver states: "I don't ask for the sights in front of me to change—only the depth of my seeing." I also prefer this soul-wise perspective, because the sights in front of me (in front of you) are in continual flux. Yet, we can learn to look *into them* to unearth their deeper truths. When I wrote *Heart Resides*, I realized I'd discovered this in the context of a prairie landscape. Something about its steady openness—its welcoming presence—had pushed me to see the value in this: as a girl, as an adult. But no matter where you reside, and regardless of the external forces that impact your life, you can choose to look at life this way. Wisdom, however, isn't a surficial phenomenon; it must be discovered within—always on a deeper and deeper level.

As I'd worked on *Heart Resides*, Eckhart Tolle, a gifted spiritual teacher, was publishing *The Power of Now* with a small Canadian publisher. Though I wouldn't discover the book until 2007 (thanks to a friend's recommendation), Tolle's work quickly drew me in on the level of knowing, and I sensed we were exploring, albeit differently, some similar spiritual threads.

I'd studied people—groups and individuals—history, culture, lifestyle, nature, customs, and especially powerful aspects of prairie landscape, from a sociological and spiritual perspective to draw out the organic wisdom of place, but on a deeper dimension, had we shared our notes, Tolle may have aptly suggested that many of my observations—points of wisdom—were indicative of awakening further from the tantalizing dream of the material world. Having grown up in central South Dakota when the world seemed less about problems, more about space and simplicity, I'd felt compelled to capture the spirituality of a vast landscape—this way of life—at the turn of the century. As I'd encountered the wise words of Thoreau, Whitman, and others, I was struck by the profound connection between their insights and what I'd experienced and observed firsthand.

Most importantly, I sensed that in returning to the wisdom of our own hearts, we would be drawn within. That is (and was) my key point: we need *something* (time and time again) to draw us inward. A place or a situation, an event or a message; a piece of art, a book, a poem, a song, a memory. An intuitive knowing. An open landscape that silently tugs at the senses—at the soul.

Granted, since the late '90s, the world has grown smaller, given technological developments; and the localized stage has shifted to an interdependent global community. Change, an intrinsic aspect of each breath, is built into each moment. But have we evolved, each of us as determined spiritual travelers? Are we more mindful, more committed to deepening our life experience?

I, for one, have never been keen on prepackaged systems for personal growth. Wisdom that is organic and commonsensical, that taps into our inherent spiritual awareness, has an authentic and powerful ring to it. And, fundamentally, since life is seldom predictable, we must draw from the curious well of experience time and time again until we find our true place within. I hope, as you read, you will find opportunities to tap into *your* wisdom, more fully, perhaps, than before, while seeing this book as a starting point for dedicated exploration that is spiritual, heartfelt.

I remember quite well my profound joy when I saw my work in print. With no idea where the journey of life was taking me—we can never know tomorrow—at least I'd paused long enough to ponder and record memorable observations about people, place, and time. More importantly, I'd bothered to care about (and showcase) something that would have been easy to overlook. The letters

Preface

I received from readers confirmed this. Here are a few of their thoughtful voices:

> *Thank you for presenting the bright side of the prairie lands. I am happy to learn to find some beauty in what was for me a land of heat, cold, dust, poverty, and trouble.*
>
> *Thank you for putting into words the very core of my existence.*
>
> *I opened your book, and as I started reading, the sounds of hundreds of people, and the playing of the grand piano in the atrium were completely obliterated. As I read your book, I knew the prairie and the people had a greater influence on me than I ever realized. My words are totally inadequate, because I will never be able to express to you how much I enjoyed your book and how impressed I am with your first book.*
>
> *What a beautiful book! It is precious to us and we so agree with your philosophy. The prairie and rural areas do offer wisdom that enriches the soul. You have said it so well. Thank you for keeping us in your heart.*
>
> *Your beautifully written descriptions of the prairie have made me homesick. It is only in South Dakota that I feel the contentment that exists and is perhaps caused by the expansive landscape.*

The Upper Midwest Booksellers Association picked *Heart Resides* as a Midwest favorite, which was a real honor;

and out of the blue, after the book's release, while we were in South Dakota, one of Oprah's producers left a lovely message on our home phone in Missouri. Well before the smart phone era, several hours elapsed before I picked up the message—we have an opening on our Remembering Your Spirit segment—so we weren't able to connect. Alternative plans were in motion by the time I returned the phone call (that was fast!); and what almost was, ultimately, was not. Admittedly, a national appearance sounded like a mixed blessing. I'd never craved a public image—prominence, visibility, recognition—although, paradoxically, all authors need that to develop a strong readership. Yet, I'm a relatively private person, a contemplative writer, content to let words on a page communicate for me; and somehow, I believe, we find the books that touch our souls. I'm sure I'm not alone when I suggest there is something inherently awkward about promoting one's book (any work of art), since creativity often arrives as a gift through simply listening to the silence that is the deep intelligence of life itself.

Every book shouldn't need to land on the *New York Times* bestseller list to be worthy: valued, meaningful, and relevant. In fact, this counterproductive orientation seems to hinder the world of publishing. Not everything in life should be quantified. Wonderful (and treasured) works of art in literature haven't necessarily appealed to a mass, or mainstream, audience. Nor should they. Rare or compelling, heartfelt or sublime, artistically unique or profoundly creative, are more lasting, evocative indicators—much better than "number of copies sold in the shortest amount of time." What is heavily marketed, trendy, or suddenly in demand, may ultimately tell us nothing at all.

Emily Dickinson was right when she said: "Fame is a fickle food upon a shifting plate." She also wisely noted: "Celebrity is the chastisement of merit and the punishment of talent."

Still, Oprah wielded real power, so with a mix of relief and disappointment, I moved on when the distant door to the promised land closed as quickly as it opened. Programming schedules shift rapidly at the national level, and luckily, I had the maturity to know there were no magic wands. Besides, just being noticed by Oprah's staff was a small miracle in and of itself.

But on another front, William Morrow (first edition) was purchased by HarperCollins about the time my book was released in hardcover, so staff and priorities shifted rapidly there as well. I'd worked with two editors—one, along with the well-respected Eagle Brook imprint, vanished.

We can count on the unexpected, on uncertainty, can't we?

As my "first book" experience continued, I also learned about the interminable life span of reviews that show up on Amazon and elsewhere (most will outlive us all). Fortunately, my goal was to write for *real readers*—those with a genuine interest in the organic wisdom of place—and that was wise, because critics rarely read the book *you* wrote. Most read, more precisely, as their life experience—their world view—dictates. And seemingly, books and articles with a spiritual or positive focus are likely to draw the illogical ire of some.

Always Returning

I commend authors for writing anyway, regardless of the external expectations of the literary world. There are numerous valid and important reasons to write a book, so deeply held personal goals should never be relinquished because of insidious elements of control that can be detected in convention, tradition, and generic reactions that have evolved historically via powerful entities in society. I studied sociology (complex organization) during my graduate years, but well before that, I believed in the wisdom at our own fingertips—in our own hearts. That's where it's found, not in the appraisal of others. Arbitrary measures and misguided standards should never replace inner wisdom. Tap into what is meaningful to you; it's always enough. And if you're an artist, a writer, a poet, remember: conformity and art are poor, if not, impossible, companions.

One spring I went to New York City to speak to the IWWG (International Women's Writing Guild) about my book. I loved meeting other authors, because we worked in isolation then, rarely enjoying opportunities to discuss our writing or the world of publishing. But life is an unwieldy dance and, since the days of becoming a new author, I've delved more deeply into matters of the spirit, especially because of a profound, life-altering loss—the focus of a new book I'm writing.

All things considered, this gentle, sustaining look at prairie wisdom deservedly meets with a new day. Sadly, some people I talked to about their experiences and ideas are no longer living—several are included in

Preface

my dedication—so it's comforting to have their wise and beautiful voices still with us in the pages that follow. Insights we call wisdom must be learned repeatedly: each time, at a deeper, more profound, level. Never, are we completely *wise*; rather, we're always in the process of becoming wise—wiser, perhaps. It's a mysterious journey without completion, and often we are ahead of ourselves: writing, listening, learning, and evolving while patiently waiting for the path to emerge more fully. A necessary leap of faith, we might say.

I hope you'll want to keep this inspirational book (not an extensive treatise on the prairies such that a Heat-Moon might write) close at hand; reading it with *new eyes* each time you delve in. We are never *finished*—not in terms of personal growth or spiritual realization. Rather, we're always returning, coming back, coming round, as our perceptions ripen: as we gather the delicate strands of our lives, time and time again.

Thanks so much for returning to this book with me.

We need abundant reminders of what we know deep within, and sometimes we need to stare down the obvious without flinching, without making life more complicated than necessary. Our minds (as influenced by people, environment, history, ego, memories, society and culture) seem to want many things (some useful, some not remotely so), but it has been my experience that our souls benefit most from the simple sustaining aspects of life that nurture our spiritual dimension.

Always Returning

So now, because of grace and perseverance and love, we return to the timeless wisdom of the prairie. A *life wisdom*, actually. Symbolic of the space within, the vast and glorious landscape of home first taught me about my physical roots, then about my spiritual roots. One led to the other as though ordained, and I'm extremely grateful that I happened to notice. Please keep noticing, deeply so, your life—the one within. It's *your place*, no matter where you reside.

Godspeed,
Daisy Hickman
September 2014

Drawing me in on a profound and memorable level, regardless of where I've lived, my prairie roots have loomed large. And I find myself always returning, literally or figuratively, to that place—to seek and share its wisdom, to remember its timeless message of survival, to find solace in its powerful presence.

INTRODUCTION
Growing up Prairie Wise

E VERYONE KNOWS WHAT IT MEANS to grow up streetwise. Yet only a handful are familiar with what it means to grow up "prairie wise"—a new concept perhaps, one we're not sure about. Some of us can picture a prairie chicken (grouse), a prairie dog, a prairie schooner (wagon) or a prairie wolf (coyote), but "prairie wise" suggests a strong link to the pioneer era. In its advanced and sophisticated state, contemporary society *surely* moved beyond this mentality many years ago. And wisely so.

Given the urbanization of America since the time of the pioneers, that is indeed how it seems—on the surface.

Yet wisdom, my primary subject, lives in the heart and soul, not on the surface, so, if we are to rediscover the power of heart in our busy lives, we must look beneath the obvious for answers. Like curious children, we must peer into the lives of our forefathers. Aspects of the pioneer and prairie creed live on in many of us, so why would we want to settle for surface explanations or faulty assumptions? The answers are rarely that sheer, seldom that vitreous.

In digging for solutions to problems that plague our world at the turn of the century and beyond, we must venture into the new millennium like spirited and dedicated explorers; we must move beyond conventional thinking by considering the old from a powerful new perspective.

We must become prairie wise.

The prairie lands represent our heritage as a people, our history as a nation—one that was built on the strength of the pioneer spirit—for it was that sense of adventure and clear purpose that moved our country forward into the twentieth century. So I cannot imagine a better place to look for inspiration, guidance, and clues to our tenuous survival as we greet the twenty-first century. Because, frankly, in our search for solutions to today's dilemmas, we may have forgotten to consider what we already know; we may have forgotten to listen to our hearts.

But the past lives on in us; we can reclaim what is ours. It is just a matter of revisiting the lands, indeed, the place, which willingly opened its arms to those who traveled before us. Our journey, however, will not be a physical one, nor will we ride in a covered wagon. Clearly, we will not confront dust storms, blizzards, or prairie rattlesnakes. Our pilgrimage will be a spiritual and emotional journey undertaken with hope, heart, love. By returning to a place that has moved many to tears, for one reason or another, we

Introduction: Growing up Prairie Wise

move forward together bravely, and with searching hearts, allowing the prairie spirit to come alive in each of us.

A commendable goal filled with dignity and purpose. But, perhaps, it is easier for me.

I grew up there—in the middle of nowhere, a common reference for prairie lands—and spent a good deal of time contemplating the meaning of life, good versus evil, the simple grandeur of nature, heavenly spirits and higher powers, the memorable beauty of mature wheat fields and peaceful stretches of deep, clear water. While I didn't understand the full value of my experience at the time, I could feel the prairie's pull on my soul no matter how far away I drifted. Like a poetic image, a magnetic force, the Dakota prairie had wormed its way into my heart in a way that defied logic and understanding.

With that as my spiritual puzzle, I pondered the prairie's beauty, its place in the world, its people and culture, until I could finally piece it all together into an informal, almost joyful, philosophy of life called prairie wisdom. Inspired by love—for a distinctive, yet down-to-earth place—by a desire to share my ideas and perceptions with those who seek greater harmony and joy in their own lives, a rough outline turned into paragraphs, then pages, and eventually, into this book. Quite simply, I felt compelled to bring the prairie to life in a positive, constructive fashion: to celebrate and share its strengths, its beauty, its lasting, and clearly powerful, influence.

Walt Whitman and Henry David Thoreau explained that companionship with nature, the mysterious, awe-inspiring out-of-doors, can stimulate a need to look inward. And the truth of their words was indeed my reality. The open land and timeless skyscapes, along with my inquisitive nature, pushed me to consider the whys and wherefores of life within the context of my early surroundings. When difficult questions emerged, I felt drawn to the prairie in a quest for answers, insight, and greater self-knowledge.

It is there where I found room to breathe.

But as I considered the powerful sentiments of Whitman and Thoreau—the words of scholars and pundits that are descriptive, poetic, and deeply inspiring, stirring our souls and imaginations like nothing else—I wondered if we haven't depended on their literary, soul-wise talents for too long, clinging to the past like frightened baby birds instead of pushing on, as we must, in a heartfelt search for what is real in today's world. For it seems our ideas have grown stale, while our hearts have hardened and our souls have grown weary. I have to believe our complacency would have shocked and saddened the pioneers, left them wondering why our nation has made so little progress in the areas that matter (equality, personal freedom, justice, concern for all human beings, meaningful challenge), especially when so many gave their lives, the lives of their children, in a quest for freedom, personal dignity, and a cherished opportunity to test their own strength.

The hardships were innumerable; illusions were few; the rewards were nearly always intangible. Yet, their path, indeed, their journey, was filled with heart; they couldn't

Introduction: Growing up Prairie Wise

have survived such steep challenges otherwise. In our search for inspiration, for knowledge, we, too, must gather our courage, moving forward like pioneers, bravely stepping beyond the forceful words and interpretations of the past, as we humbly ask the prairie for more.

This isn't an easy task.

The place itself, the prairie and its culture, speaks softly, whisperlike at times, so it can be difficult to capture its essence. Glorious, yes. Splendid and breathtaking, as well. But also stark, expansive, surreal. It's all of this, and more. To me, to my prairie heart, the terrain I grew up with evokes feelings of pure delight. Untouched and free, the prairie symbolizes the great unknown—past, present, and future wrapped in one, a convincing space knowing no boundaries or limits, no worries or demons: a place where my heart resides.

Yet, I'm also reasonably certain that these lands, this place, does not impact everyone in precisely the same way. There have been times when I resented the prairie, everything it stood for, everything it seemed to ask of me; there were also times when I misunderstood its firm grip on my heart and soul. But in coming to terms with its lasting influence, I'm finally able to articulate its value, its essence, for you, and in so doing, I realize just how far "we" have come together: the prairie and I. Like friends who have survived the good and the bad, growing ever stronger through the inevitable struggles, disappointments, and challenges life offers, the prairie and I have weathered the storm together, and at long last, it won my heart.

Always Returning

It can be difficult to speculate on the feelings of others, however.

Many who grew up with the prairie, many who live there now, rarely speak of its role in their lives—its curious force and quiet strength, its simple demands and rich rewards. Like sacred ground, the prairie is cherished quietly, without fanfare or formal proclamation, as the land commands a good deal of reverence and respect, much like the oceans, outer space, or towering mountain ranges.

The urgency and complexities of daily life seem to fade in this context.

The landscape encouraging contemplation—while drawing something pure, surprisingly charming, from us. Something we didn't suspect was there.

Walt Whitman wrote a prose poem as he crossed the Great Plains in 1879; published in 1882, "The Prairies and an Undelivered Speech" appeared in *Specimen Days*. "But if you care to have a word with me, I should speak it about these very prairies; they impress me most, of all the objective shows I see or have seen on this, my first real visit to the West. I wonder indeed if the people of this continental inland West know how much of a first-class art they have in these prairies—how original and all your own—how much of the influences of a character for your future humanity, broad, patriotic, heroic, and new?"

As Whitman correctly senses, the prairie lands, with so much to offer, can be equally difficult to comprehend or appreciate with any degree of success or satisfaction; they can frustrate, subdue, provoke. Decked out in its natural

Introduction: Growing up Prairie Wise

grandeur, safely hidden from the public glare in the heart of South Dakota, the prairie tucked itself into a way of life that has grown up around it. Like a happily married couple, the people and the prairie have become one.

Indeed, it's a good place for our journey to begin. By focusing our magnifying lens on the very heart of the prairie, we all can find room to breathe.

Always Returning

If there was a road I could not make it out in the faint starlight. There was nothing but land: not a country at all, but the material out of which countries are made.

~WILLA CATHER,
My Antonia

CHAPTER ONE

A Dance with Destiny

Here, starting with the origin and value of an informal philosophy based on the nuances of place, people, and time, we begin our spiritual journey into the private, well-preserved folds of the prairie and its culture. In myriad ways the prairie is a place filled with possibilities, a place where the heart resides; and when you take the prairie, its people, into your heart and life, no matter where you live, you will sense the quiet strength, the peace and the power, of a landscape that has, historically, brought men, women, and children to their knees—deftly, without regard for race, religion, age, stature, education, or gender.

In the eyes of the prairie, we are equals, no matter what.

Of course you may want to mold the finer details of this prairie-wise philosophy to your individual needs, personal preferences, and life circumstances, but the prairie's essence (the profound sense of inner awareness one notices in gazing upon it) supersedes and surpasses state lines, city limits, and neighborhood cliques. Fortunately, getting to know the prairie is a function of the heart—an orientation transported without plane, train, or automobile—and prairie wisdom is a set of beliefs that transcend, join, and inspire. The prairie and its culture are more than a place on a map. There are only around 845,000 people in South Dakota; yet, *heart* can't be quantified.

You need not live here to benefit, that is part of its mystique. Rather, the wisdom of the prairie, like a precious stone, can be carved out in the form of words, pictures, and concepts that reach out, touch the heart—the seat of passion and change, and all we hold dear.

William A. Quayle wrote in *The Prairie and the Sea*, "You must not be in the prairie; but the prairie must be in you. That alone will do as qualification for biographer of the prairie. . . . He who tells the prairie mystery must wear the prairie in his heart."

As one who wears the prairie in my heart, I am eager to share its mysteries, so regardless of where you reside, you can carry its inspiration with you. Should you have an opportunity to visit or live here one day, so much the better, but as my final chapter explains—it's okay to come and go. Prairie life isn't for everyone, nor should it be; its purpose, as the pages of this book reveal, is much greater.

The prairie's teachings are universally significant and globally intriguing. Wisdom that is born of the heart can be modified to suit individual proclivities; it can be used to nurture the dreams and desires of people of all ages and walks of life. For love is the great unifier, the energy that contains enough passion and power to change lives—inspiring us to great heights, moving us to tears of joy or great pain, motivating us to examine our beliefs and values, or make the compromises of a lifetime.

Whatever your destiny, goals, problems, joys, or challenges, a little prairie wisdom along the way—a window to the heart—will serve you well.

Physical Roots

We all have a beginning, a place we call home. For me, it was growing up on the prairie—on the plains of central South Dakota. And while I don't remember my first encounter with the land, nor my earliest impressions, I recall the open spaces being *all around me,* and I also remember spending time outside with my grandmother in her yard exploring flowers, heaps of walnuts, and the lily-white blossoms on her apple trees every spring. Somewhere along the way, maybe as a girl or a teenager, maybe later on in life, when I was in college and traveling home to see family and friends, the prairie made its presence known to me.

In contrast to what I experienced in central Missouri—I did my undergraduate work at Stephens College—the prairie was undeniably different.

The air, in Columbia, sometimes sticky and damp, created a thick haze, a musty smell; the sky seemed distant, not as compelling; the rain was intense and frequent and trees seemed to be everywhere, while the winds were often mild, a light breeze to me. And the winter came and went without much notice at all. But what bothered me above all else, I could never seem to find the sunset or the sunrise, not in the same way I'd seen (and experienced) them in the open spaces of home. Too much was in the way, too much came between me and the sky.

I felt cut off from the beautiful surroundings I'd known, and taken for granted during my youth, by silent barriers. Everything seemed watered down—less vibrant and intense, not magnetic or thought provoking, less magical in its ability to comfort and inspire, to lift my spirits with images of the great unknown. I was a "stranger in a strange land," as Thomas Wolfe put it in *Look Homeward, Angel,* and as reflected in the title, *Stranger in a Strange Land,* a science fiction book written by Robert Heinlein.

While some wouldn't have taken note of the geographical and societal differences to the extent I did, for me it was a strong signal to dig deeper, to figure out who I was in relation to this new land, this place, *not of the prairie,* that seemed to want to overshadow and hide the very things I'd grown to love. My search "to understand" followed me: no matter where I lived, no matter what I did, refusing to be ignored, refusing to let me rest for long. But in my quest for answers, in my willingness to ask tough questions that tease and taunt us like merciless riddles, I learned to live with ambiguity. And I learned to value the process, the ongoing search for truth and understanding that had come to define my life.

The prairie had presented me with a puzzle of life-size proportion, and in my attempt to solve it, at times letting

A Dance with Destiny

the various pieces sit idle for a while, just simmering in my mind, something pulled me back time and time again. And though I wrote this book to complete the picture, I assume nothing, knowing the prairie, the ideas it has forced me to consider, probably has more tricks up its sleeve.

Still, I'm taking this brief interlude in my life journey to bring to light useful prairie teachings because the message of the prairie is really quite cosmopolitan. In pausing to consider those who preceded us, our history as a people, as a nation, indeed, where we are headed, it is helpful to glance backward and inward. Wise to search our hearts and souls for answers. It's from this perspective that we turn inward, because to become prairie wise you must be willing to know yourself more deeply; you must be concerned about emotional, intellectual, and spiritual survival in today's somewhat wearisome world.

As you have probably gathered, prairie wisdom is about learning to look, really look, at life in a way that spotlights the inconsequential, peers under and below the shiny, glittery surface of things, delves into the dusty corners and invisible crevices in an effort to understand the truth of the matter, indeed, the heart of the matter. There is plenty of time for that on the prairie—fewer people, fewer distractions—so it naturally invites questions and serious contemplation about the things that matter: self-discovery, hope, kind deeds, integrity, love, courage and conviction, and whatever else is on your list. With equal fervor, the land, plain and understated, seems to downplay materialism, pretentiousness, false and largely destructive judgments that fail to honor the humanness in us all.

William Least Heat-Moon in *PrairyErth (A Deep Map): An Epic History of the Tallgrass Prairie County*, a monumental book about the prairie lands of Chase County, Kansas, writes this: "I came to understand that the prairies are nothing but grass as the sea is nothing but water, that most prairie life is within the place: under the stems, below the turf, beneath the stones. The prairie is not a topography that shows its all but rather a vastly exposed place of concealment . . . where the splendid lies within the plain cover."

That isn't to say that the prairie is a perfect place, nor are its inhabitants. But without a doubt, it's a different kind of place, one that doesn't reveal its treasures easily, yet one that can draw out the best in you, forcing you to go beyond absolutes, black-and-white thinking: superficial distinctions that alienate and divide. While my state's history is speckled, like a child's Easter egg, with good and bad, holy and evil, birth and death, it's rich and powerful at the same time—offering an incredible opportunity to sort through the many complexities and contradictions of life. But even as it provides a mesmerizing framework for purposeful observation—the creation of a philosophy that is refreshingly commonsensical—I, and the world around me, are continually evolving.

This wisdom of place seeps into my heart, peers around the corner when I least expect it, and I sense my inability to capture it "all." Yet forge ahead we must; as wisdom, in any tradition, by any other name, is far from an exact science, and in sharing my experience and understanding of these windswept lands, a deep honor that has brought me to tears on numerous pages, it's my hope that each of you who read this book will derive something unique from the prairie's essence: insights, novel ways to apply the ideas and observations tucked inside this book. We are in this journey together, and each of you will have something worthwhile to contribute; maybe you'll be inspired to consider what "used to be" and "what is" from a new vantage point.

The past lives on in our hearts, and as we reconnect with parts of ourselves that were lost or misplaced, ideas once discarded or tossed aside will resurface. A bit like hearing from an old friend, our eyes may light up, our minds may buzz with thoughts and memories, and our hearts may reach out for more.

Most of us know more than we think we know—a good deal of which has simply been forgotten. But luckily, the prairie, the place and its people, has not changed much.

Still there, patiently waiting for our return.

It's a good time to rekindle the warm fires of old, to reconsider the wisdom that already resides within our hearts: maybe dust covered or slightly misshapen, but there nonetheless. Reading on, you'll encounter:

Humor, history, and intriguing connections.
Ideas revisited, renewed, updated, or clarified.
Colorful quotes from experts, or students of the prairie.
Wise and wonderful insights inspired by nature.

Passages painting a vivid picture of the prairie landscape.

As Thoreau noted in his journal entry for December 31, 1841: "In society you will not find health, but in nature. You must converse much with the fields and woods if you would imbibe such health into your mind and spirit as you covet for your body."

Prairie Dimensions

The prairie lands I know most intimately are situated in the very heart of the prairie, but, first, let's get our bearings. South Dakota may look square, basic, and deceptively consistent on a flat paper map, but the state cradles two distinct sections: East River, West River. The split designation has been around as far back as anyone can recall, yet there is nothing more than friendly rivalry between the sides.

Geographically, the state isn't large enough to withstand too much inner turmoil. That, and a good deal of old-fashioned pride, keeps Dakotans basically unified. Likewise, each side of the state has its share of tiny, pebble-like communities that are nothing more than a fleck of dust on the planet's surface. What you will find in these small towns is simple: a few trees, probably cottonwoods; a grocery store of six to ten rows; an old gas station; the corner post office; and a few residential streets attached at the sides or in the back, much like an afterthought.

Places like Ipswich, Mud Butte, Epiphany, Isabel, Glad Valley, Badger, Hub City, Ralph, Buffalo Gap, Olivet, Fedora, and Crow Lake dot the horizon along with towns like Red Elm, Prairie City, Long Lake, and Bonesteel. It's a mesmerizing mix that almost imperceptibly paws at the imagination, and like a rake against dry grass and brittle leaves in the fall, just hearing the names of these unpretentious communities stirs the soul.

What is there? What is behind the town's name, if anything? What are the people like, and what in heaven's name do they do all day? Why are they there; what do they believe? The names are colorful, somehow majestic in their simplicity, and as a matter of reference, many of these towns are situated smack dab in the middle of the prairie, probably within a stone's throw of open grassland.

Otherwise, towns come in all shapes and sizes, culminating with Sioux Falls, the state's largest city. With an approximate population of 150,000, it's located in the southeastern corner of the state. Rapid City, a West River community, is the state's second-largest city. Located in southwestern Dakota, Rapid is a lovely mountain town that connects to the Black Hills and is only a few miles from Mount Rushmore.

This is the touristy part of our state. With Crazy Horse—the world's largest sculpture at 563 feet high, 641 feet long, and supervised by sculptor Korczak Ziolkowski until his death in 1982—forming on Thunderhead Mountain (near Custer), along with the revitalization of Deadwood, a beautiful mining town made famous during the gold rush of 1876, the western section of Dakota is destined to grow.

Always Returning

In the central part sits Lake Oahe—and one of the world's largest earth-rolled dams—the state capital, numerous Canadian geese that winter on Capitol Lake (warmed by an artesian well), and countless pheasant and deer. Pierre is the small community that holds the pieces together. That's where I grew up in the late fifties and sixties; a beautiful river town of about 14,000 people, the area is a fishing and hunting haven. Hunters fly in from all over for the annual Governor's Hunt, a pheasant hunt held each fall. A good guide service can do quite well.

Lodges, some are quite impressive, spring up wherever wildlife abound; from primitive to elaborate, prices for a "gun" tap out at around $2000 for a three-day weekend.

With the beautiful Missouri River framing Pierre's southern boundary, it's commonplace to own a boat. Some kind of boat, any kind of boat. Referred to as the walleye capital of the world, fishing is a popular pastime, and tournaments of national distinction draw fishermen from all across the country. Weigh-in ceremonies are well attended. And each spring, when fishing is at its finest, the sparkling river waters, especially in the early morning hours, are dotted with boats of all sizes, shapes. For some, fishing is serious business; for others, it's carving out time to relax. For me, it was a bit of both. Not learning how to fish until my late thirties, I remember my dislike of worms. Minnows weren't as much of a problem, however, so when silvery walleye were biting on jigs and minnows, those were better days.

A Dance with Destiny

And what a thrill, catching my first walleye. The small white tip on the end of the tail, the memorable eyes, its sleek contour. It was an exciting moment, one that never grew old, even when they were biting no matter how inept the fisherman. I soon learned to watch the river for clues. The "walleye chop" is when the wind causes the water to roll and toss in easy, lilting waves. This is when you should drop everything and go fishing because, under these conditions, the movement of your boat is well camouflaged from the elusive walleye.

Another popular way to fish on the Missouri is to pull plugs (poles baited with a "wally diver" perhaps and cast out the back of the boat as it trolls down the river at a steady clip). But this method, I didn't master.

Interestingly, though, when asked where I grew up by people who haven't experienced this part of the country—the sparkling river, the windswept prairie—their reaction is often predictable, slightly entertaining. "Anything much to do there?" they inquire with a slight frown, or "Does everyone drive a pickup truck?" Maybe, "I bet that's a good place to get a pair of cowboy boots, maybe a cowboy hat." They might also inquire about the snow or the wind, but one question predominates: "Do you pronounce Pierre, Peer or peeair?" And so it goes, until I wonder why no one asks a good question, one that might cause me to stop and think for at least a minute or two.

If you are also curious, "Pierre" is pronounced *peer*.

Technically, since the town's origins are French, the correct pronunciation is *Peeair,* but Dakotans prefer to say "peer" nonetheless.

A discussion of Dakota wouldn't be complete without mentioning our notorious climate. Famous for its extremes, it's a toss-up as to which is worse, winter or summer, because both seasons can be quite intense—from dreadfully hot, dry summers to bitterly cold winters. On the whole, many winters are long-lived with blowing snow, steep drifts, below-zero temps, all of which make going outside somewhat unappealing, if not impossible. I remember plenty of hearty blizzards when a look outside revealed nothing more than a blinding white blur.

We lived in town then, where the wind was slightly less free, but I still couldn't see across the street. The ferocious wind, sometimes fickle and unnerving, is part and parcel of prairie life. Much has been written about prairie winds, the one constant during all four seasons. Windmills, in all semblances of repair, continue to dot the horizon.

Wileta Welty Hawkins, a family friend who passed away in 2008, said: "When I moved to South Dakota in 1943, I thought I would die! No trees. And the wind!"

And, yes, we talked about the famous author, Eudora Welty, and she thought there was some connection. Wileta's father was William Welty.

No doubt, the wind is a force to be reckoned with, but nature reigns supreme where I grew up, the wind merely the persistent messenger. While it is ridiculed by outsiders and insiders alike, most people tolerate prairie wind with a certain amount of aplomb: It is there for a reason.

Evenings begin to cool off by late-August, but summer days are incredibly long.

There is nothing exactly like a summer evening on the prairie—quiet and mystical, the stillness and the waning light can seep into your soul. But there are also plenty of raging thunderstorms, some rather nasty, in fact, while rain, in general, is sometimes scarce. When it finally lets loose, even as a delicate, short-lived sprinkle, there is cause for celebration.

Hail, however, is cause for concern. Often dropping from the sky with the force of a high-speed drill and very little warning, for farmers hail spells trouble, if not a big loss.

Spring can be a glorious season, especially when *some* rain drops from the sky. That is when the prairie comes to life with free-flowing wildflowers; sometimes tiny and timid in appearance, but often vibrant in color, prairie flowers make their dependable debut at a time when nature seems to be proudly announcing its winter survival. And this spirit, vivid and real, is somehow contagious: a time to share in nature's joyful resurgence, to greet another growing season with a grateful and expectant heart.

And, finally, there is autumn.

It can come early and is best described as a mixture of lingering summer days, early winter, and something in-between. I remember when a Halloween snowfall caught plenty of us by surprise. As a general observation though, autumn's arrival is greeted with mixed feelings: the hot days of summer are over, but the cold winter snow will fly again soon. If I pause to imagine a prairie fall, fields of gigantic drooping sunflowers come to mind, along with images of massive combines gently roving the countryside against a blazing red-orange sunset. Add to that a wonderful earthy smell. Rich and full, it's a stout mix of grain, prairie dust, and late-blooming flowers like golden chrysanthemums and burnt-orange marigolds. A powerful aroma that fills the senses, stirs the soul, with feelings of completeness and contentment, a prairie autumn, once experienced, can produce a hearty string of memories to hold close as an organic, lasting source of inspiration.

The Prairie and Its People
So who are these people, the people who, out of choice or circumstance, live in the middle of nowhere? Are they as mysterious as the place, or have they merely become one with the land? Do they love feeling isolated from the world, insulated from "city problems," or do they sometimes sense they could be missing out on all the excitement?

Curiously enough, all of the above are true.

Dakotans (Dakota, in this book, refers to South Dakota) are surprisingly diverse in their viewpoints, and individually, as unique as any other population. Yet, there are tendencies and general patterns that effectively supersede the differences, perceived or factual. Like the East River/West River debate that rages on as a matter of habit, many differences are superficial. In fact, there is a common bond that supports a noticeable spirit of strength and cohesion, and when you look closely, you'll find similar beliefs and values.

When the chips are down, as some say, they rally around each other like family members. A measure of loyalty comes with time, shared experience, and mutual dependence, and you can find a good number of old-timers who wouldn't move if their lives depended on it. The area gets its share of new, or almost new, arrivals, too. Some are escaping city life; others yearn to rediscover their roots; and some land in Dakota because of a spouse, a job.

Depending on the situation, transitions are smooth for some, while others endure tedious months of culture shock.

Those who return to the area after a prolonged absence often marvel at how little things have really changed during the past five, ten, or even twenty years. Change does occur—the latest fads and conveniences eventually arrive—but only in due time, and not because there is significant demand for either one. Whatever represents change, *anything considered new*, is sprinkled on top of the old very lightly and usually only as an afterthought, never as the main dish. There is too much fondness and genuine appreciation for what is already here.

Many of the prairie's people are quietly in love with a way of life that has existed for a long time; it is as if they sense their uniqueness, the very specialness of the area. Yet such sentiments are rarely discussed, not openly anyway. Many residents tend to be modest, and relatively private. Some are afraid that too much talk might be detrimental to their lifestyle, which, for many, is considered a small luxury; many simply prefer that outsiders admire the area from a considerable distance.

That is not to say that Dakotans are an inhospitable bunch. The majority simply value what they have—some consider themselves spoiled—and most would like to avoid problems of the big-city variety. So, in many ways, parts of the state are in a preservation mode, which often leaves people feeling threatened by outside influences. Yet therein lies an economic and real-world dilemma: Nothing stands still forever.

Within any system or organization, eventually there must be change and growth; basic survival depends on it. But a deep reluctance, a clear resistance, to new ideas and ways of doing things isn't uncommon. Prairie dwellers also read newspapers, watch television, travel, and listen to the radio. They know what it is like "out there." And while some of it may look enticing and sound appealing, for the most part these people, young and old alike, favor the status quo.

In general terms, living on the prairie is relatively safe, comfortable, and reliable, and while certain career opportunities aren't readily available, and from a strictly economic perspective, most salaries aren't impressive, many residents believe these "facts of life" are a necessary trade-off, one they are willing to make. A general lack of resources is accepted as part of the area's heritage, and even though residents may complain about it periodically, many are wise enough to understand that limited financial resources aren't the same as a spiritual or intellectual deficiency. In fact, materialistic limitations may be responsible for some special qualities, the ones money can't buy or simulate.

That very dynamic is in keeping with Thoreau's thinking.

"Do not trouble yourself much," he says, "to get new things, whether new clothes or new friends.... Superfluous wealth can buy superfluities only. Money is not required to buy one necessary of the soul."

If right *then*, he is even more accurate today.

We see the resurgence of his thinking all around: books on caring for the soul, articles about doing with less to find true happiness, movies that feature a return to heart and soul, an amazing variety of self-help tapes telling us to throw off financial concerns in exchange for peace of mind and spiritual growth. Yet this is not new thinking on the prairie; this is a way of life. Growing up there, as part of my particular and individual dance with destiny, I learned at a fairly young age to view materialistic gains with a cautious and skeptical eye. Plenty of people seemed content, joyous, and complete with the simple things, and those with significantly greater resources, the minority, no doubt, didn't seem any happier.

Material wealth doesn't seem to be a guarantee of anything. Not just in Dakota either, but in every place I've lived. Life is, and always has been, more complex.

Character comes in all sizes, shapes, and colors. Happiness comes from within. And peace of mind, that rare and glorious commodity, is something each of us, regardless of external circumstances, must work at achieving and maintaining each day.

Prairie Wise

This was my framework, my perspective on life, when I left the safe confines of the prairie. Fortunately, I took with me a strong sense of identity, plenty of self-respect, and a quiet sort of confidence nurtured by life in a small town on the prairie—my experience of its culture, my companionship with the land, the sky, the river. I'd also learned to question the obvious, to look below the surface of any situation for a deeper truth, a more meaningful reality.

If we take the time to look, to perceive, and to care, discovery is within our grasp. Most things are not what they seem—more or less maybe, yet different from what superficial observation suggests. Perhaps this is why I pursued a graduate degree in sociology. Intrigued by prairie life, the modern-day version included, ever since I ventured out into the world as a college student, I felt prepared to study the science of society. I'd learned firsthand that a seemingly poor state was, in other ways, rich, because of its intrinsic value—because it's a place where the heart resides—and I'd also discovered parts of myself, at a relatively young age, that, had circumstances been largely different, might have been difficult to find at any age.

I'd heard about hard times, about the trials and tribulations of the pioneers, but of even greater interest: stories of survival. Those I heard about, those I witnessed. When problems looked insurmountable, many people simply dug in—radiating a "can do" spirit that helped them prevail no matter how bad things got. And there was such pride in accomplishment; I saw that, too. From a great crop in autumn, to a new baby or a bountiful garden, life in its average, everyday form, seemed to be enough; being without a new car, a new anything, was rarely cause for alarm or dismay. Of course I'd also learned that these same people—the ones who often inspired me—were not infrequently looked down on by outsiders who didn't understand, or appreciate, the inherent richness of their ways.

Disparaging references weren't uncommon.

But no, I decided, not true, just warm, down-to-earth people with heart—people taking things one day at a time, usually with a "grain of salt." Old-timers had seen too much, experienced too much, to worry about sophisticated ways, and a good number of them had inherited a strong, independent spirit.

"I ignore people who try to boss me; I believe in equality and think I should have my own say-so." With a noticeable twinkle in her eye, Wileta Hawkins also advises: "To make the best of things, no matter what."

My appreciation for the prairie—its flavor, its history, its culture—is strong and clear. And though I've lived elsewhere, and despite times when I was living in Dakota and feeling closed in and closed off by the prairie's bewildering expanse, when I ponder the ways of the world, I'm increasingly grateful for the diamond-in-the rough-opportunity I had growing up there: in a place that may be closer to heaven than many care to imagine.

Always Returning

    As I came to realize, growing up prairie wise was a special chance to learn about life on a fundamental level by offering a rare look at what is and isn't important—something that can take a lifetime to figure out. Thus the prairie spirit runs deep in my heart and soul.

    I carry it with me no matter where I go, no matter who I meet or what I do. Especially useful in today's society, with its plenitude of distractions, multitude of ways to avoid and hide from reality, legion of false definitions of success built into a fast-paced society to the point where values and priorities have been distorted, twisted, and abolished, where many have simply given up, and where many are looking for an easy way out, a shortcut through life offering nothing but bliss and good times, I cherish the consistent lessons of land, sky, and wide-open space. Oddly enough, with all we have created as a global society, genuine happiness seems more elusive than ever; just when we believe we've found *it*, we begin to complain when our wonderful sense of discovery fades. When it all begins to feel strange, empty, curiously nondescript. Slowly slipping through our fingers. But still, the mindless chase goes on, happiness falsely equated with comfort, status, and possessions, when such distinctions serve to block our human view, keeping us lost and floundering. Effectively, at bay, from more meaningful pursuits.

    When one new car doesn't work, buy another. When the latest house doesn't suit, get a bigger one on a much bigger lot. And when the newest, most fashionable clothes don't work either, try a better watch, a couple of big-screen

A Dance with Destiny

televisions—maybe a swimming pool. That isn't to say it's wrong to desire or accumulate objects that can bring us pleasure, but as the unencumbered prairie lands seem to whisper: when you expect artificial things to create and sustain happiness, disappointment will ultimately follow. Life, in its many dimensions, is so much more. And genuine happiness, like everything else, must be based on knowledge of self, a willingness to endure difficult times, and an ongoing commitment to what is real.

As Frances Nickel Jones, age 104 in 1999 (and now deceased), said: "I guess working that hard must have agreed with me." Frances, a homesteader near the Bad River area of west-central South Dakota in the early 1900s with Louis, her husband, experienced more hard times than she sometimes cared to remember, but very little truly got her down.

For starters, when Louis died in 1928, she didn't give up.

She and her two young sons hitched up the horses to go to church; chopped river ice for the cattle; cut and hauled enough river-bottom wood to last an entire winter; raised turkeys and shipped them to Chicago by rail; survived dust, grasshoppers, and prairie rattlers. Yet despite it all, Frances was a happy, spirited woman. Her eyes twinkled; she listened to what others had to say with interest and concern; she often had something insightful to say. And, amazingly, Frances didn't bother to sell her house and move into a group living home until she turned 100. A local celebrity due to her age and joyous nature, Frances Jones, her life and her personality, were a strong manifestation of the prairie spirit. Her life was tough but, like the prairie, she survived. And Frances was indeed prairie wise.

She agreed that the easy life was little more than a vacuum, a big, black hole that neither sustains nor rewards. A testament to the prairie, of all it teaches, Frances was magical in inspiration. Her happy spirit may outlive us all.

Like the majestic prairie lands, she seemed to want to say: *Wake up! There is more to life than you think.*

First, though, we must find the time, the lasting willingness, to dig into life instead of skimming along the surface with unfocused busyness. Delving into a perspective that results in doing more of what counts—less of what causes us to lose our way—we will be closer to envisioning a road map to the heart. A clear destination, one propelling us forward with the stalwart intentions of a pioneer in a covered wagon, is critical. Then we may discover, as we step forward, a plenitude of wisdom leading to a more hopeful, more peaceful, world. At the very least, to a more inspired (and understandable) world.

Why should we live with such hurry and waste of life? We are determined to be starved before we are hungry.

~HENRY DAVID THOREAU,
Walden

CHAPTER TWO
Open Space

THERE IS A PRAIRIE ANTIDOTE to the frenetic pace, the maddening pressures, of everyday life: practice the fine art of doing nothing. Perfect it, if you can. Build it into your day, your way of life, your game plan for success, and don't wait until you are unable to do anything—an entirely different situation. Unless you've carved out an exceptional lifestyle, you are probably burning the candle at both ends, as they say; you may even be moving at the speed of light, dancing faster than you like. This is a common predicament, one that has plagued mankind for decades, and while we all wish for greater balance in our lives, rarely are we able to live up to our own expectations. Seldom do our most admirable intentions see us through.

Think in terms of practice—it helps.

Always Returning

Change comes gradually and only with long-term commitment; resistance is guaranteed. Yet even under the best conditions, you may be incapable of doing less, so doing nothing is next to incomprehensible. You try to settle down or calm down, but your mind, your body, won't let you rest; your family and friends won't let you be; your restless soul won't let you tarry, or even pause to fully enjoy your surroundings—the people or the place.

It's understandable. Programmed from birth by society, workplaces, and those we love to act and react, perform, produce, prod, push, and pull, we are merely falling in line with the explicit and implicit desires of those around us. Over and over again. The prairie, however, offers an enlightened alternative, one that teaches something true, something powerful: doing less paves the way for doing more. This insight—highly suitable for our harried times—comes through loud and clear on a visual level.

A thoughtful survey of the land reveals a place, *a space*, basking in a nearly timeless state, as if suspended in a magical potion. Vast stretches of flat land, gently rolling hills with slopes and curves of seemingly artistic origin, wide-brimmed sunsets, wildlife that scurry around like self-important diplomats, lazy skies extending high and long above the fray—above our daily plodding—and dusty gravel roads without beginning or end.

Try to imagine it. Let the word hurry fade and disintegrate into a virtual blur.

The unspoken message is obvious: Hectic schedules, a hurry-up, do-it-now mentality, cannot compare or compete with the persistent beauty and quiet strength of the prairie. As we scramble about each day, dashing here, dashing there, the land does the opposite, and without a word speaks directly to our souls, touches our hearts, and reaches out, like a laser, to connect with our finer, more discriminating sides. In the overall scheme of things, even our best efforts to stand out above the crowd can only be seen as less than monumental in comparison to the elegance and stature of undisturbed land, remarkably free of man-made artifacts. Still, in an attempt to make our mark, to get everything done, we get caught up in a vicious cycle of do, do, do, hoping the end result will justify the means.

For you, it might.

For others, though, this continual round of going and doing, initiates a truly exhausting, mindless motion that rarely, if ever, ceases despite noticeable feelings of fatigue, sadness, and incredible stress.

With enough repetition, constant activity—for the sake of activity alone—can begin to feel natural or even necessary, yet unexamined busyness is a clear road to nowhere, one that results in doing less instead of more. By the time we figure this out, however, the clock may have wound down, and maybe only belatedly do we realize how we failed to stop, look, and listen—when we had the chance, when the time was ours—how we failed to prioritize *after* consulting our hearts.

Unfortunately, given our culture, it's quite easy to assume that being busy is inherently important, while doing nothing on purpose is the equivalent of being lazy, dull, worthless, or depraved. *Not so.* And it's not that people who live on the prairie believe in doing nothing to the exclusion of pursuits that really do matter. It's just that in a place where nature and common sense dominate, there seems to be an intuitive awareness that the human body, and indeed the spirit, need time, permission, and encouragement to do less.

Curiously enough, doing less often translates to more: more time to recharge, to regroup; to stay in touch with important feelings, values, beliefs, and, of course, other people; to let situations and events unfold naturally, at their own pace; to do what supports our dreams, so we might grow old gracefully, knowing few stones were unturned.

Where connections to others run deep, where everyone knows everyone, it takes a plenty of down time to nurture such relationships. Growing up on the prairie, I grew accustomed to friendly exchanges that were casual, comfortable, and unpredictable, and while fortuitous encounters of the small-town variety may seem insignificant, they actually meld the fabric of daily life by creating a reality that is neither contrived nor high pressure. When your day is jammed full of must-do, can't-wait items, there isn't time for casual exchanges; there is little opportunity for the unexpected, unplanned, spur-of-the-moment cup of coffee with an old friend, the walk to the park with your son or daughter or spouse.

Still, these are activities that contribute to a way of life that promotes the importance, the fundamental value, of the human connection: without fail, without exception, without excuse. That's why it's considered *important* to go fishing, take a walk, enjoy a spectacular sunset, help a neighbor with some badly needed house repairs, plan a birthday party for an aging (and unsuspecting) relative. Prairie picnics are also a priority, along with "stopping in for coffee." And card parties, usually whist or gin rummy, are a dependable social highlight.

While such activities aren't the equivalent of doing nothing, time must be available for such pursuits on an "as needed" basis; time that is given freely, shared without resentment, keeping score, or feelings of regret. When this happens, as it does on the prairie, there is a wonderful flow, a gentle rhythm to each day—a dynamic that allows events to unfold in an unpredictably comfortable manner. And there's a strong sense of give and take: increasingly difficult to find in our overly competitive, urgent world. Within this context, much is gained. For one thing, a lifestyle that supports people!

If that sounds strange or simplistic, consider the dehumanizing events of your day or week. Do you notice them? Is that how you *want* to live? What are we doing to ourselves, now and over the long run?

A Leap of Faith
But how, you may ask, can doing nothing be considered an art form? Isn't it mostly a matter of crossing off the less important items from a lengthy, out-of-control list? Yes and no.

Successfully doing nothing is a true art form because it requires us to dig in—study our lifestyles, evaluate priorities, consult our hearts and souls, elevate our minds, discipline our well-worn habits, adopt new and novel ways of thinking, contain (and hopefully understand) our weaknesses. Moreover, a "do less to do more" orientation challenges most of us because it sounds deceptively easy, when it actually requires active (purposeful) decision making. And pushing us to make difficult choices, it yanks at our guilt strings, and may cause us to feel silly or inept. It may also cause our friends, families, and neighbors to *wonder* about us.

Then, of course, there is boredom to deal with, hyperactive impulses, irritability brought on by self-imposed restraint, and frustration from not seeing the immediate benefit or value of doing less. We live in a world of instant gratification, which implies action, speed, and tangible results. So, indeed, *doing nothing* is an art form that requires practice and patience. As for crossing items off a list, we know how long that age-old tactic lasts—a day or two.

Ultimately, if you are to use this well-known aspect of prairie wisdom, you will need an open mind, a considerable amount of thought and imagination, a determined attitude. Like so many things, it may require a leap of faith. For encouragement, you might remind yourself: the less you do, the more you'll do—of what counts, of what makes you feel alive and growing, of what helps you become a fully realized human being.

More than anything, *consistently* doing less is a mindset, an adventure, a commitment—all of which requires a stout heart and a willingness to take a stand.

Open Space

A New Image

If you live in a mega-city where the pace is truly relentless, or if the whole idea of doing less, and thereby more, sounds remote and abstract, something you cannot quite put your arms around, take heart. While the demands of contemporary society can and do take their toll, sometimes causing the most "together" individual to feel overwhelmed, confused, or frustrated, it's still possible to create a new, improved image—a more rewarding lifestyle, a happier spirit. And if the hectic pace feels comfortable—if you manage to keep all the right balls in the air, if you don't feel that stress is a major problem—that's fine, too, but over the long term, a grueling, never-stop lifestyle will most likely catch up with you.

So even if you're that unique someone who claims to experience no excessive pressure from the complexities of daily life, it's not a bad idea to consider how your lifestyle choices will manifest over time. Creating a life is a bit like designing a magnificent sculpture in your particular image, and good or bad, polished, lopsided, or incomplete, it's still your image. For a comparative reference point, consider the prairie's image for a moment.

Is it one to emulate—one to cherish, to absorb, and to protect?

Walt Whitman described the prairie like this: unbounded, unconfined, combining the real and the ideal, as beautiful as dreams.

That is quite an image.

And if the prairie lands are indeed beautiful, then Thomas Moore, the author of *Care of the Soul,* would surely approve of their influence and image as well. "The soul is nurtured by beauty." And "What food is to the body, arresting, complex, and pleasing images are to the soul." Moore goes on, "If we lack beauty in our lives, we will probably suffer familiar disturbances in the soul—depression, paranoia, meaninglessness, and addiction. The soul craves beauty. . . ."

The key, however, is his definition of beauty.

"For the soul, then, beauty is not defined as pleasantness of form but rather as the quality in things that invites absorption and contemplation." Content and form should be arresting and ". . . lure the heart into profound imagination."

The prairie, known for its magnetic pull, its harmonic overtones, sounds like good food for the soul.

Coming Full Circle

The settlers, the pioneers, traveled to the prairie more than 100 years ago; indeed, it was a time of exploration and expansion, the prairie lands providing ample opportunity for both. Only now, our nation has come full circle (and is presumably still coming full circle one day, one event, one historic moment, at a time). In the interim, we've learned that less is more—precisely what the prairie implies and offers.

As we return to these lands through the pages of a book instead of as pioneers in a covered wagon, we seek many of the same things: inspiration, spiritual awakening, a fresh start, an opportunity to rediscover our potential, a chance to put the heart back in our lives. Clearly, the time is right for reflection. It's important that we somehow journey back to these distant and isolated lands to honor and preserve the prairie culture, to rediscover its truths, to unearth its full bounty. And this book, fortunately, offers a unique opportunity to revisit, as pioneers of the twenty-first century, the unassuming place that became "home" to many of our forefathers: this place where the heart still resides.

Based solely on the grandeur of nature and simple, soulful ways, the prairie's wisdom is profoundly emotional, intelligent, and life-enhancing; so even if you never get a chance to experience this place firsthand, to study its splendid texture over time, prairie wisdom, when defined and clarified in contemporary terms, can become part of your life, too. While that may sound impossible, it's not.

When we are attentive, genuinely aware, and deeply in touch with our surroundings, we can draw an organic kind of wisdom from our surroundings; we can share it with others.

Discover Your Truth

Allow more "open space" into your schedule—indeed, into your life—and you will be one step closer to finding your way back to your heart, *to your truth*, and one more step away from the short-sighted, self-serving ways that tend to predominate in contemporary society. And while the

Always Returning

first step may be the hardest, to prevail is the prairie way, to forge on is the pioneer spirit. Is it alive within you? Do you sense its pull, its place in your heart?

These are the gardens of the desert, these
The unshorn fields, boundless and beautiful,
For which the speech of England has no name—
The prairies.

~WILLIAM CULLEN BRYANT,
The Prairies

CHAPTER THREE
A Steady Beat

YOU HAVE AN INTERNAL CLOCK—one that says slow down, move on, take your time—but how often do you consult it, how often do you quickly dismiss it? How often do you run right over it in a vain, misguided attempt to stay in control of, reasonably on top of, an almighty schedule? Nearly *all the time* you may be thinking. We are all in this predicament, together.

Fortunately, there is still something called prairie time. If you visit, you'll notice it right away; if you live there, you're most likely in tune with it already, and wouldn't trade it for crates of gold, barrels of oil, a lifetime supply of apple pie or chocolate cake. Not now, not ever. On the prairie, time is rarely rushed or based on impatient attitudes. Rather, prairie time is sweetly balanced, rhythmical, and flexible; as we have already seen, it even allows for the unexpected. Like a godsend, prairie time is based on natural, internal states, deep human longings too readily ignored and denied in a world that wants everything yesterday and waits for no one.

Once you understand the prairie's organic rhythm, its place (always evolving) in our world, yet another commonsense tenet of prairie wisdom is unearthed: build a bridge to yourself. Its importance is obvious. When you are out of step with your private rhythm, you are, in sum, out of step with yourself, and most assuredly, you are out of step with the cosmos.

Still, we may push on, relentless in our pursuits, shortsighted in our vision, cut off from the vitality of our spirits. When this is the case, is it any wonder our activities lack heart—at work, at home, at play? Or any wonder that, as a whole, so many people seem disillusioned, exhausted, forlorn? Out of deep frustration, we tend to question everything from the basic values that made our country strong to the fundamental need to care for our emotional and spiritual needs in a world that says: *There is no time.*

To heal ourselves—our nation, our world—we must have the courage to consider where we have been and where we are going. More than anything, we must build a better bridge to ourselves. Slowing down enough to savor the absolute richness of life, all the wondrous things happening around us, will help restore our hearts; it will open the door to what is locked inside each of us—help us envision new solutions to lingering problems of old.

A Steady Beat

The first step: consult yourself, your well of internal wisdom. You don't have to be old or graying to possess wisdom. Too often discounted as a meaningless hunch, inklings or ideas that quietly bubble to the surface at unpredictable times or come in sudden waves of knowledge and insight may also be personal wisdom seeking expression. Admittedly, it's easy to ignore intuitive nudges, and it seems that inner wisdom is sometimes confused with nonconformity. Then, sadly, our more useful, unique insights aren't given serious attention, even though wisdom, a revelation that may not be explainable in concrete, rational terms, knows no rules or boundaries. Perhaps that is why skeptics treat notions of wisdom with suspicion or outright contempt. If something—an idea, an impression, an approach—falls outside a known (mainstream) paradigm, it must be false, useless, or ridiculous, right?

It occurs to me, however, that since the heart is inherently wise and knowing, could it be, *could it be,* that in shutting down our hearts to protect ourselves from pain, in closing ourselves off from the world and its many problems, we are unintentionally blocking the natural flow of wisdom from entering and therefore, from bettering, our lives?

Do heart and wisdom go hand in hand—how could they not?

Let's return to the idea of an inner clock, to something called prairie time.

While the settlers often complained of loneliness, of long, dreary days filled with silence, worry, and sorrow, when they recorded their memoirs as Walker Wyman did for Bruce Siberts in *Nothing but Prairie and Sky: Life on the Dakota Range in the Early Days,* most were eager to share their stories, remembering the very "sweetness" of their lives. Siberts was seventy-seven when he contacted Wyman to help him put his thoughts and recollections together, and during the five years that followed, between 1945 and 1950, he produced over 900 pages in long-hand; by then he was eighty-two. And although he died in 1952, two years before the book was published, Siberts surely would have treasured the end product, a charming and illuminating memoir of his life on the prairie from 1890 to 1906, as edited and prepared by a Wisconsin State University professor of history.

Homesteading near Plum Creek, a few miles west of Pierre, South Dakota, in West River country, Siberts lived as a bachelor in a crude shack for more than fifteen years, and even though life was clearly hard, "filled with doubts about the wisdom of trying to wrestle a living from the land," soon the land and its spirit were in his blood. A bit like falling in love, his words reveal how deeply he came to care about the place and its people.

In 1894, when he caught a free train ride to Chicago to visit his sister, Siberts decided to stay for the winter, but he didn't last, and soon enough concluded: "The Chicago people were a bad-mannered lot. They would shove and push each other around in a pretty bad way." He headed home on the train and was happy when he arrived. "The air was good, and with all their faults, I liked the Dakota people." Siberts also discloses an acceptance of time and self in relation to prairie life. "After a summer herding horses in South Dakota a man can get as much prairie and sky as he can stand. When that time comes, he has to go to town and blow off some steam, sit in the shade, and talk to some other human beings. I was in that shape in August 1899, and started out early to do something about it."

What did Bruce Siberts know that we may have forgotten; what sort of inner wisdom was he consulting?

As Wayne Fanebust writes in *Tales of Dakota Territory*, within a chapter titled "Mystery of the Bones," "The land of the bright sun had a dark side. Like an unpredictable temptress, nature drew in the unsuspecting and unprepared. . . . Many of whom became her victims." The prairie wasn't for the fainthearted. To survive, people had to take note of the forces created by nature and circumstance that demanded their attention; they had to know when they couldn't take any more solitude—any more prairie and sky—and that meant staying in touch with their inner world and the one around them.

In other words, they had to work closely and willingly with Mother Nature, not against her—respecting her time line, her imposing presence—as nature didn't allow inhabitants to call the shots. To peacefully coexist with nature, the pioneers had to develop a sixth sense. They had to display a willingness, an ability, to conform to the wishes and demands of a power they couldn't match, understand, or conquer. And they had to manage their personal needs in relation to the same unbeatable phenomenon.

In short, they had to build a bridge to themselves by considering their unique rhythms and impulses, but they also had to be in sync with the realities of prairie life. For sure, the pioneers had to learn how to bend with the demands of unseen forces, as prairie time, in a class of its own, didn't fall in line with their requisitions or expectations.

Yet it's such a natural dimension that most people of the prairie wouldn't want to keep time any other way. Prairie time provides a cybernetic bridge, as people become one with the land, thinking and acting in rhythm to its steady beat.

Rosemary Radford Ruether, in *Meditations from the Wilderness* edited by Charles Brandt, writes: "Return to the land means recovering something of the biorhythms of the body, the day, and the seasons from the world of clocks, computers, and artificial lighting that have almost entirely alienated us from these biorhythms."

So for good reason man-made time lines aren't an overly serious matter where life with the land is commonplace. There are, of course, exceptions to everything, but most people sense the ultimate power of the "big clock," which means no mad scramble to get there first. And only the naive believe they can "beat the clock." But as you have probably concluded, that's good. People gladly succumb to the hypnotizing effect of the land, and in return, the open space, the gentle grass covered hills, act like an invisible force, shielding, protecting, its inhabitants against the debilitating "hurry up and do it now" thinking of contemporary society. Why do we act as if life is a race?

A Steady Beat

The ultimate beauty of this orientation, however, is that there is often time—to dream and reflect, to listen and observe, to discover your natural rhythm, to do less . . . to do more. Essentially speaking, there is time for matters of the heart. There is even time to doodle, a commonsense prescription for getting in touch with yourself. If you know how to draw and create genuine art, feel blessed, but for most of us, producing silly pictures and meaningless creations resembling absolutely nothing—plain old doodles—works almost as well.

The process, like the journey, is important, not the results.

Anything will do—pens, pencils, crayons, Magic Markers, whatever is handy—and feel free to write on napkins, scratch paper, old newspapers, phone books, even the sole of your shoe, if that is all you can find. But when you create art, even something very simple (even a doodle), your mind switches to neutral by focusing on something harmless and restful, and in that primitive act, you create a time cushion. Nothing more than tiny, thin slices of time, a time cushion is a place where you, and you alone, can pause briefly to get in touch with your internal clock. The prairie lands offer a similar remedy.

By providing a cushion—spacious, absorbent, comforting—the land shields inhabitants from the harshness and excesses of modern-day society. Time seems irrelevant when you gaze out at tall grasses waving back and forth with abandon, at a sky larger than life. As if time stopped long, long ago, no skyscrapers can be found.

Always Returning

The prairie is an island unto itself, in a multitude of ways, and even though time-keeping mechanisms are everywhere, their impact is questionable—their efforts to control residents nearly futile. For many, time is something to be considered in the Thoreauvian sense.

As he wrote in *Walden:* "Time is but the stream I go a-fishing in. I drink at it; but while I drink I see the sandy bottom and detect how shallow it is. Its thin current slides away, but eternity remains. I would drink deeper; fish in the sky, whose bottom is pebbly with stars."

When time is scarce, when pressure to-do and to-hurry is everywhere, try your hand at a doodle or two, especially when you cannot find any other way to put the charm, or the heart, back in your life—when you somehow managed to blow up that bridge to yourself instead of strengthening it.

In fact, in January of 2014, on CBS Sunday morning, I caught an intriguing Lee Cowan segment called "The Higher Purpose of Doodling." The theory is: "doodling is a window to clarity." In Cowan's interview of author Sunni Brown and professor Jesse Prinz, his guests suggest that: doodling isn't a mindless activity, but instead engages the mind in a way that helps us think. And Brown's website (she offers doodling workshops) offers more evidence via new research of the value of doodling.

"Using common sense, experience and neuroscience, Sunni is proving that to doodle is to ignite your whole mind—and she'll teach the world how to master 'strategic doodling' in her forthcoming book, *The Doodle Revolution*."

A Steady Beat

In 2007, a book was published about presidential doodles. Reportedly, John F. Kennedy often doodled sailboats; Ronald Regan, cowboys.

I know of another very creative guy, author Hugh MacLeod, who began doodling on the back of business cards while sitting in a bar. Those images led to a blog, a book, and a global-wide business that focuses on creativity.

I've been a doodler for as long as I can recall. It's great to let the mind wander and see what turns up. When I wrote this book in '98, I had no idea there would be a national doodling revolution in the years to come. I guess I was ahead of my time.

We come and go, but the land is always here. And the people who love it and understand it are the people who own it—for a little while.

~WILLA CATHER,
O Pioneers!

CHAPTER FOUR
Habits of the Heart

Magical in nature, rituals thrive in small prairie communities. While many are simple and unadorned, these practices build meaning and purpose into life. Sometimes they mystify; sometimes they redeem. But without these absorbing, enjoyable, other-centered activities, life can take on a barren, colorless flavor. Besides, there's something about repetition that prairie dwellers appreciate. It's part of the wisdom of place.

One charming woman, tiny, brimming over with vitality—even in her eighties—baked fifty-some pies every summer with apples from her own tree just for the sheer pleasure of giving them away to friends and family. A man down the street froze enough rhubarb to last a lifetime, then put an ad in the paper and gave most of it away. Yet another prairie dweller stayed up half the night making pickles and baking kuchen for friends and neighbors.

There is something earnest about the prairie lifestyle—something that encourages the pursuit of activities that, when repeated, become heartfelt, soul-enriching rituals. On the surface, such habits of the heart could appear to be less, even eccentric, but wise inhabitants understand the human need to reach out, to share what they have with others. It's like an organic spiritual practice—to repeatedly do what seems curiously simple yet rich in spirit. Why? Because of personal commitment, because it feels authentic, because it matters.

Many residents also understand the wisdom of letting their hearts guide their decisions. In a world that produces a good deal of pragmatic, logical, cost-cutting deals, how refreshing to consider a place where people still value people, where the process doesn't take a backseat to the end result. Not automatically, anyway.

Consider, from a prairie perspective, the informal gathering of farmers and ranchers at a country coffee shop. Maybe they are perched on short bar stools, hats on their heads. Or maybe they are huddled in a booth, crowded around a small table. Those arriving after six in the morning are greeted with remarks like: "Sleepin' in again, are ya?", "Somebody sick in the family, wife got the flu?", "That old truck givin' ya trouble?" And after a few well-meaning snickers, a contented sort of chatter sets in. Dead of winter, early spring, summer, late fall. It's always the same.

Early morning coffee—usually black as night—in a small cafe with whatever name you care to imagine. While I've never been to a cafe called The Main Stop, I can picture such a place, such a scene, on just about every surviving main street in small-town South Dakota. And no matter how many times this scenario repeats, in no matter how many unpretentious-looking prairie cafes, a type of communion occurs.

Without fanfare, without undue planning or preparation, men, maybe a few women, in ritualistic fashion, meet near dawn to gather and draw strength from their shared lifestyle—their steady companionship—to share stories of home and family, and to renew bonds of faith, loyalty, love. While almost always unspoken, noticeable caring radiates from their camaraderie; concern springs from their conversations; each day now a tiny bit brighter, each individual's journey somehow lighter. What about the early morning walk, the evening stroll to the ice cream shop, sitting by the river to study a spring sunrise?

Uncomplicated pastimes, when repeated, take on special meaning and quiet purpose. Reminding us of our ongoing need for stability, predictability, and soul-wise pursuits, such routine activities comfort our frazzled nerves, repair our often frayed, twenty-first-century heartstrings, and help us sustain a connection to each other, to ourselves, to the world.

A Prairie Picnic

I remember well a family picnic to celebrate spring. Nothing elaborate, nothing contrived, just: let's go celebrate the arrival of a new season after a long, gray winter. We met on the banks of the Missouri near Lake Oahe, winter's snow, dusty and frozen and still visible by the shoreline. Our unpretentious gathering included your usual picnic foods, a small blaze in a public grill, warmish jackets, and easy conversation. The nurturing effect on our sagging winter spirits truly spectacular. But we were people of the prairie, and our expectations were reasonable, simple, ordinary. Something that helped any event succeed.

That is another important dimension of this lifestyle.

Rituals that sustain our hearts and souls are best enjoyed and appreciated when low-key in design. By asking so little of us, the return is considerable. For one thing, prairie rituals often involve nature and the vast outdoors; sometimes they involve the inspiring ways of other living creatures. One soul-wise woman rises early in the morning, especially in the spring, to watch and listen to the birds.

Like Thoreau, is it possible that she, like other prairie dwellers, believes in a perfect correspondence between the inner nature of man and the structure of the external world, between the soul and nature? Nature, to Thoreau being the materialization of spirit and a physical realization of divinity, referred to it as sacred, worthy of man's respect and awe. As he wrote in a chapter called "Solitude" in *Walden:* "There can be no very black melancholy to him who lives in the midst of Nature and has his senses still."

Not surprisingly, the prairie itself can seem like nature's belly. The unassuming lands, poetic and sometimes wistful in bearing, encourage people to notice all of nature: its rich display of color, its contentment, its triumphs and its sorrows.

Too often discounted as trivial or trite, the genius of nature is evident in the middle of nowhere. There is less competition for limited and overburdened attention spans, so people take note of events, ceremonies, even parades, that nature, and nature alone, provides. And as we watch, rituals of magical, if not mystical, proportions come into focus. They are born, sustained, and, quite literally, handled with tremendous care.

Heartfelt Sayings

The power of words, noted for centuries by scholars around the globe, is no less important or compelling on the rolling prairie. The people, the culture, and the place are set off by a vernacular that silhouettes the lifestyle while accenting the intrepid nature of the genuine Dakota native. A few fad-type words penetrate the screening process, but overall, "talk" is down to earth, no-frills needed.

Fast talkers, smooth talkers, or, heaven forbid, talkers with a pretentious air are suspect, and when scrutinized by the longtime resident, it's clear the "locals" are nobody's fool. They value honest communication, a straightforward manner, a friendly demeanor that feels genuine and true. Within this context is a built-in appreciation for words that inspire. Heartfelt sayings are passed down through the generations like gems worthy of belief and preservation. Providing a path for the young, the newcomer, the lost and confused, prairie sayings, some old, some new, add depth and pizzazz to most any conversation.

Were popular sayings part of your life, part of the wisdom of a place you knew well? Although framed by years now vanished, do they color your memories—run through your mind when least expected?

The Early Days

My grandmother's favorite expressions, "Keep the peace" and "Keep a song in your heart," come to mind for me. An authentic prairie woman born Christmas Eve of 1889 in Cuthbert, South Dakota, she was also fond of saying, "It will all come out in the wash."

A short, stout lady with little regard for fashion or foolishness, Anna outlived all but one of her seven siblings, coming to her final rest two days shy of ninety-nine. Her advice, her encouragement linger on, finding purpose, earthly renewal, in the pages of this book. I was born on her birthday, on Christmas Eve. She would have applauded my efforts as an author. From an early age, I loved to discuss the ways of the world with her.

Much like the endearing prairie, Anna's lifestyle—her love of nature, her commitment to family and humankind—is timeless in its capacity to inspire me. And even though she talked about the prairie fire that destroyed their newly built frame home when she was in her teens and her father's unexpected death before his fortieth birthday, her outlook was usually sunny in a genuine sort of way. I could see it in the way she lived, feel it in the way she looked at me, hear it in her words. A predictable, uncomplicated routine, her soothing gaze and gentle speech, reflected a softness born of strength. I believe she possessed a deep and abiding contentment—felt at peace with herself and the universe—and openly delighted in the joy of others.

Some seemed to envy these qualities; others seemed confused by her calm, accepting nature. But as a young girl, I felt drawn to it. Her manner gave me silent reassurance that everything would work out okay—that no matter what, she would be there.

Anna's love was constant, abiding, like steady sunlight; she seemed to harbor no malice of heart toward anyone. I admired that most about her. With no illusions about hard times—she'd endured plenty—Anna remained true to her prairie spirit until the end. Loved life for what it could reasonably offer, while finding consistent refuge in nature.

Her garden brimmed over with hollyhocks, pink, white, red, and purple. And I recall so clearly her tall, stately, walnut tree; her bountiful blackberry tree; her apple trees amidst the changing seasons; the everyday habits of robins and squirrels. Anna also found comfort in her music, playing the piano and the violin by ear.

Seated at her old upright, her wrinkled hands performing without fail, she would begin with a rousing rendition of "Turkey in the Straw." Then "When Irish Eyes Are Smiling" or "You Are My Sunshine." I loved to sit beside her. When I was a young piano student, she often listened to me practice. I can also see her now as she paged through a thick volume of Alfred Tennyson's poetry—another one of her treasures I yearned to understand.

From this bountiful existence came a happy heart.

Made famous by the children in her neighborhood—she loved to share the apples from her trees or build a small bonfire in her yard for marshmallows—Anna cherished the underling. She took pleasure in using her resources wisely so others might benefit. And through her kindness, she inspired others to keep going despite setbacks or loss; through her words and deeds, her wonderful prairie heart lives on. Not given to self-pity or indulgence, as I watched her live, I saw the value in making the best out of things.

Yet she is not the only one to understand the importance of living well—to be at peace with nature, your surroundings, and those around you; to share wisdom, caring, and love; to make acts of kindness a priority, allowing others into your heart unconditionally.

Most of us can repeat a few heartfelt sayings passed down through the generations; they are part of what knits our lives together, keeping us in touch with ideas that never seem to grow stale. They can bring us down to earth when our common sense has disappeared like a strong March wind—when we overintellectualize a problem, deny our feelings, forget our hearts and souls. The prairie culture, in particular, keeps such sayings alive and circulating; new ones are born along the way. Some survive the test of time.

Habits of the Heart

As I talked with longtime residents about their favorite phrases—many are universal—I kept a short list to share:

Friends are good but family is what counts.
She has nothing to do and all day to do it in.
Into every life a little rain must fall.
A place for everything, and everything in its place.
Waste not, want not.
Watch the pennies, the dollars will take care of themselves.
Always carry on, the best you can.
Leave it to Mother Nature.
Keep the spirit.
Good fortune is a matter of perspective.

And from A.B. "Bud" Tyler, Jr., (1910–1999) internationally known polo player and family friend: "The nicest thing you can give anyone is a smile; it doesn't cost a dime."

We must march my darlings, we must bear the brunt of danger,
We the youthful sinewy races, all the rest on us depend,
Pioneers! O pioneers!

~WALT WHITMAN,
"Pioneers! O Pioneers!"

CHAPTER FIVE
Almost Anything Once

IN A FLOURISHING contemporary society, options and choices, things to do and see, places to go, are endless. Especially true of urban areas, where no matter how narrow a particular interest, others are there with the same one. From finding a group dedicated to yoga or poetry or the martial arts to locating those who like to ski-dive, scuba-dive, or drive a race car, look online, read the newspaper, or ask around.

Remote corners of the world, isolated villages, teeny-tiny towns, and, of course, prairie-based communities, including those who reside miles from another living soul, experience a different reality: a narrow menu, a short availability list, an "outside the mainstream" set of options. In such contexts you might not find a formal class on archery, mountain climbing, how to play the harp or the bagpipes, the history of ragtime, Buddhism, or anything else your imagination conjures up on the unique side of things.

You might, though, find an informal group dedicated to square dancing or learning how to waltz; you might find a fishing class or a horseback riding club. Maybe a few people like to hunt for arrowheads; a group of historians might be committed to the art of storytelling. With any luck you can find a few people dedicated to books, art, hunting, boats, gardening, playing cards, cake decorating, knitting or sewing, walking, swimming, or aerobics. Maybe. But some places on the prairie are so completely remote (desolate, in the eyes of some) that you won't find any of the above. Farms, ranches, and homes can be thirty to sixty to ninety miles away from anything besides a lonely tree at the end of a dusty gravel road. Isolation that is crushing if you pine for the companionship of anyone (or anything) besides a family member, a cherished pet, livestock, the land, or nature.

O.E. Rölvaag's classic, *Giants in the Earth: A Saga of the Prairie,* begins, "To those of my people who took part in the great settling, to them and their generations I dedicate this narrative." The loneliness of the prairie comes through in riveting detail: "In the dead of winter, of course, when the blizzards are raging and we don't see any folks for weeks at a time, she has days when she seems to go all to pieces; but I hardly reckon that as the disease—that sort of thing happens to a good many of us, let me tell you!"

But for a more recent description of prairie life: "When you are born on the edge of the plains, you spend your life clinging to it, praying that you won't fall off."

Almost Anything Once

Appearing as an essay in *Leaning into the Wind*, a work edited by Linda Hasselstrom, Gaydell Collier, and Nancy Curtis, contributor Robyn Carmichael Eden also writes: "But we are stubborn optimists, never thinking we won't survive. The land is our trial, our comfort, and ultimately, our identity."

In the same book, Katherine Wood shares this in a poem called "Plains Preponderance": "Then the dry spring wind comes up billowing dust across the farm-perfect view, swirling dirt against the Jeep, making her feel desolate, almost crazy for no reason." Wood goes on, referring to the dust as a "layered curtain of prairie gold" while conveying a strong sense of continuity: Has the prairie experience really changed over the years? Sod huts no longer dot the landscape; herds of buffalo no longer roam freely across a great expanse; and the Native American culture has undergone a tremendous amount of change. The horse-and-buggy era is barely a memory. Yet the prairie's essence seems largely untouched.

It still features many of the same things: a sparse population; a people, who, as a whole, are of a kind and friendly nature; a vast space that is mostly unfenced, generally uninhabited. Nature, weather, livestock and grain prices, rough-and-tumble politics, hunting and fishing are still the name of the game. At least, for many.

Driving on an isolated road, gazing at an endless stretch of prairie, noticing how the intense sky dominates the entire scene, and maybe catching a glimpse of a renegade pheasant can bring tears to my eyes even though

Always Returning

I grew up with the prairie at my side. Never tiring of its comfort, only feeling puzzled by its constant pull on my heart and soul, to me the prairie, the lifestyle built around its mystical and mesmerizing presence, the entire package—people, place, history, and culture—remains, even today, curiously poetic.

In the sense that there is a beautiful rhythm to the unchanging yet dynamic landscape, to the prairie's knowing spirit, to its uninhibited nature; in the sense that I love this place: this place where my heart resides.

Change is a relative commodity where I grew up, and generally speaking, time marches on with little to no effect on the place itself. You are right to conclude that scarcity is often the general rule. So you probably won't find (excluding a handful of communities slowly becoming cities) an extensive list of functions, activities, clubs, and entertainment outlets prepackaged or arranged just so.

Therein, however, lies the nugget of wisdom that is the focus of this chapter: try *almost* anything once.

A Slightly Different Menu

One of the most intriguing aspects of prairie life comes to light within this framework, this idea of trying the unplanned, the unexpected, or the undesired at least once. Because of the outward limitations imposed on the area due to geography and otherwise, life on the prairie seems to demand it. Those living here strive for creativity and resourcefulness as a matter of habit, frequently tapping into those traits when deciding how to spend time with friends and family, or when sharing resources, developing interests and hobbies, and simply looking for *something* to do.

But some, those who haven't been here long, prematurely conclude that the prairie lands are stark and barren: seriously lacking in opportunity. They haven't figured out that it's just a matter of being open to a slightly different menu. Fewer *obvious* options and choices isn't the same as an utter void. When open to trying new things at least once, self-discovery lies right around the corner. And as many of the pioneers must have believed, an adventuresome spirit can spell the difference between stagnation, an existence devoid of heart and joy, and true happiness. Even with motivations that were necessarily varied, even complex, these men and women seemed to sense the inherent value in reaching beyond the safety net of a world that was rapidly becoming settled, orderly, and predictable.

The lure of the great unknown, a powerful force indeed, led them inward, geographically and spiritually. And so it is now, as pioneers of the twenty-first century, that we still travel inward to console the places that feel lost and unsure, nearly numb from the excesses of modern-day society, practically frozen from fear, frustration, and strife.

Luckily, life-enhancing clues remain on the prairie. A place that embraces, requires, and supports a lifestyle that is outside the mainstream invites us to look more closely, and when we do, we are offered a different vision. So instead of running from its foreign qualities, its subtle shape and unique contour, because we assume the prairie's time has come and gone, we have much to gain by submerging ourselves in its mysterious currents. Then we are more likely to notice the inherent limitations of prepackaged activities that are supposedly novel, flamboyant, or exciting.

Regardless of age, gender, lifestyle, or income, doing *strange* things—charting a creative course, digging in to find new possibilities—is conducive to a happy heart, a strong mind, and a vital spirit. But if options are excessive, if choices are never ending, we can drown in our own abundance. It makes sense after all.

Like impressionable children skipping through bright, tantalizing, candy stores, saying no becomes increasingly difficult, and while those who suffer from having too much don't know which way to turn, those who suffer from having too little feel ashamed and dejected, like aliens on a planet they no longer understand or appreciate. But by offering simple fare, a back-to-the-basics approach, a prairie lifestyle can reduce the painful gap between too much and too little, allowing the "inevitable classlessness of prairie life" (Heat-Moon, *PrairyErth*) to exert itself.

Within this "flattened" terrain and perspective, many have learned to stay open to a way of thinking and behaving that keeps them growing and young despite the perceived limitations of the local menu. They have learned to "try almost anything once."

Newcomers

Those who move to the area from drastically different environments, even some who are returning home, may come to this understanding slowly as opposed to quickly. A few truly panic at the sight of such a "thrown wide open" landscape; others frantically try to re-create what was customary for them in another place, another land, another time.

As Robyn Eden points out in *Leaning into the Wind:*

> *In the vast prairie hyperspace, there is no room for clutter. Those who call the prairie boring and empty are those who pass through quickly, moving from one densely inhabited place to another, senses so dulled they need the neon gratification of mountains or seas or deserts. Born into a world of sensory overload, they are blind to the low-light vision of the plains. Used to perpetual motion, they cannot stand still long enough to feel the pull of roots just below the surface of the undulating grasslands.*

But Eden admits that: "The human offspring of the prairie are different at birth. Others spend lifetimes desperately seeking what we are born knowing."

How true it is that newcomers are sometimes overwhelmed by the basics, confounded by the lack of readily apparent options, and, quite frankly, annoyed by a lovely simplicity. One woman, after moving here from a city, said: "I felt like someone had dropped me right off the face of the Earth." Referring to her new residency in a remote part of South Dakota, you can be sure she speaks for others as well.

But eventually a transformation occurs.

Always Returning

The disgruntled (or perplexed) newcomer, after sinking into the lifestyle for a time, discovers surprising merit in the perceived strangeness—in their personal encounter with an annoying emptiness. With all that that implies, this category of *change* can be truly eye-opening. What is the catalyst, you ask, or is it merely about holding still for a while as the prairie works its magic on your heart, your soul?

In my humble estimation, conversion of this magnitude stems from a convergence of forces not easily isolated or understood. But for starters consider the eventual realization: The prairie, the people and the lifestyle, must be appreciated for what they offer, not disliked for perceived shortcomings. This kind of acceptance can take time, especially for those who are resolutely opposed to making the transition. But once this development takes hold, the "city person" cautiously ventures out to the Fourth of July day rodeo; or maybe he picks up a fishing pole for the first time; quite possibly, she decides to learn how to play whist (a popular card game). Or maybe someone offers to teach her how to make chokecherry jelly, how to dance to a country tune, how to ride a spirited horse in the next parade down Main Street. Everyday pastimes are made brand new: a joyful process in every sense of the word. For newcomers, you can almost see the welcome relief; you can certainly feel it.

While it *may* be less than an actual rebirth, this liberating process of letting go, of staying open to trying almost

Almost Anything Once

anything once, is more special than some suspect. As we experience something new—engage in activities we actually resisted—we may also notice the evolution of surprising abilities; we may notice how dormant interests rise to the surface once more.

Initially, this organic, almost imperceptible, transformation may overwhelm you in the most positive sense. Like a surprise you never expected, your heart may race, but if you are truly wise, you will come to a point of gratitude for an experience that forced you to reach inside for a new reality, for bringing your spirit to life once again in unpredictable ways.

Watching children playing in the snow, their joyful squeals immediately capture your attention. Your heart. You smile or wave; you nod in appreciation for their happy state of mind. Maybe you reach down to make a snowball of your own, then toss it toward a nearby tree just to watch it splatter and fall to the ground. Quite simply, it's fun. And trying new things can also be fun. As a bonus, as you nurture an interest along, it may gracefully evolve into an absorbing passion that stimulates growth, happiness, inner peace—all forms of personal wealth.

In the guise of nothingness, the area, gently but persistently, suggests that we consider things anew. We may as well, because as you now understand, *that is all there is*. But in relinquishing a touch of our stubbornness, surrendering to that which appears strange or lacking, we may come to understand ourselves better.

Always Returning

We may even feel rejuvenated and joyful as we once again realize that less is more, a powerful, prairie-wise belief. Most important, as we let the prairie's wisdom seep into our hearts, we may see the road map a bit more clearly: *this road map to the heart.*

*The silence of the Plains,
this great unpeopled landscape of earth and sky,
is much like the silence one finds in a monastery,
an unfathomable silence that has the power to re-form you.*

~KATHLEEN NORRIS,
Dakota

CHAPTER SIX

Weathering the Storm

Have you tried to imagine a world with less noise—a world without chaos, confusion, or corruption? Where might it be found, what might it look like, why might it exist? Most important, what might you do there?

Such private musings, common to most, reveal our innate need for calm; they underlie our ongoing search for what is real. In many ways, a desire for greater harmony and peace in our everyday lives is reminiscent of daydreams, of graceful, delicately swift butterflies flitting around in a dreamy display of color. In contrast, our movements and actions, in capturing our human limitations so grandly, appear uncoordinated and slightly inglorious. We limp; we sag; we sometimes drag about like poorly performing puppets.

How could we not yearn for a smoother existence—forever imagining a more tranquil setting in which to play out the limited days of our lives?

People of the remote prairie lands—past and present—may know a reality more along these lines. And while it's not a carefree existence in any way, a degree of natural serenity is bound to emanate from acres of native grasses accented by a seemingly heavenly light—reams of golden rays, or by night, a blanket of brilliant stars—wildlife, wildflowers, and stretches of clear, clean water. Inviting, peaceful, and otherworldly.

But for those who settled the land, a first encounter with the prairie sometimes caused them to venture "timidly into the edges of the grass," clinging to the "outriders of forest like mice hugging a wall. For this was alien land, not only in physical appearance but in its harsh rejection of familiar custom; it diminished men's works and revealed them to a vast and critical sky, and forced people into new ways of looking at the land and themselves, and changed them forever."

John Madson, in *Where the Sky Began: Land of the Tallgrass Prairie,* goes on to write: "The world had opened into a light-filled wilderness of sky and grass that would open its people as well, freeing them of certain dogma, breaking old institutions, and shaping new ones to fit the land." That was then. Now, however, as we come full circle in our quest for new territories to explore, this "alien land" reaches out to us like an old and deeply trusted friend, quietly calming our fears, gently whispering our names; a beacon of light stretched out before us. A place that has weathered the storm. Time and time again.

This inner awareness—how incredible, how important.

What was once a source of fear has come to mean much more. In fact, we find ourselves cherishing what is left of the great prairie lands, clinging to them as though their death may somehow precede ours. Like a final visage of the past, symbolic of our desire to stretch as a nation, to advance, when the prairie is gone, something deep within us may cry out with a shrillness of heart: *Don't leave us behind.*

The Inside Story

But how has the prairie wormed its way into our hearts, with us barely noticing? And how has this transformed us in the process?

Wayne Fanebust, in *Tales of Dakota Territory*, described the prairie as a "place nature created to test the brave and crush the weak and foolhardy."

What an intriguing description.

Regardless of its challenges, even with its bumps and blemishes, many have come to love this place. Indescribable beauty played a role, as did a powerful sense of freedom. A famous settler, author O.E. Rölvaag, in *Giants in the Earth*, captured the breathtaking beauty when he aptly described the western sky near sundown with phrases like "luminous with splendour" and "radiating a glory not of this world."

Obviously, the prairie offers its own brand of rewards, encouraging those who live here to come to terms with who they are and what they believe. You can't hide from the prairie; you can't hide from yourself. And eventually, if you stay long enough, you join hands with the land—its glorious side, its dark side, its side you don't quite understand. This union, the dynamic it creates, has a particular effect on residents, causing some to appear "dry," even a bit crusty; it's as if the intense seasons, tough times, and dusty roads have taken their toll.

Prairie people, a unique lot to be sure, can be unnerving, especially for outsiders who aren't at all accustomed to their ways. Baffled by their calm exteriors that seem to be matched by equally serene interiors, by smiles that are often slow to surface, by a casual attention to material effects, some decide, albeit prematurely, that prairie residents are jaded or provincial. No, not really.

Most have just figured out a few things along the way.

One woman who lived in the central part of Dakota for sixty-four years said she grew to appreciate the plains with their ever changing light and the way it danced on the landscape. One senior citizen, 101 when I wrote the first edition of *Heart Resides*, explained how life on the prairie taught her about the value of long-range views. And Frances Nickel Jones, at the proud and noble age of 104, explained to me how the prairie had taught her patience.

In 1920, one gentleman, in writing a letter (as excerpted in *Where the Sky Began* by John Madson) described the considerable effect of the plains this way: "It had taken the shrillness out of them. They had learned the trick of quiet."

Even today, even now, the prairie can have a similar effect, somehow bringing us closer to ourselves. Like a gentle backdrop to our running-around-always-busy ways, the prairie delivers a sense of stability, natural beauty, and peace. It helps us learn the trick of quiet, as so well explained more than ninety years ago, and from this expansive perspective, a great deal can be learned.

In fact I'm reminded of the ants and the bees, furiously at work to ensure their survival. When we finally grow quiet—when we pause at least briefly to reflect and ponder life—its wonders and mysteries, its force and power, its magical way of taking us exactly where we need to be when we least expect it, we begin to understand how we are a reflection of those ants and bees. And in this funny, mirrorlike dimension it's even more apparent how stately, how surprisingly grand, the prairie lands look in comparison.

We also can't help but notice, within this telling image, the sharp contrast between deep, abiding calm and perpetual zaniness (as our daily routines appear); clearly, there is much to be gleaned. Much that is well beyond the obvious.

A Quiet Sense of Purpose

Look inside your soul, inside your heart. Did you find a sense of peace or one of panic? Feelings of confusion, chaos, or calm? Joy or pain? While the answers may be strangely elusive, they are usually there if you listen—if you truly want to hear them. But when was the last time you stood still long enough to really probe the depths of your heart and soul; did you like what you found?

Those who reside on the prairie for any length of time, by conjuring up internal visions of that which surrounds them in their everyday life, seem to be magically in tune with their inner resources: their heart and soul, the truest of true, the internal barometers we sometimes ignore in exchange for external indicators lacking precision, courage, and wisdom.

Like the cowardly lion in the *Wizard of Oz*, we are taken in by razzle-dazzle fads; scared of anything that wakes us in the night; and leery of the unfamiliar, the unknown. *We look to others to lead the way.* Mostly because we are captivated by the wrong indicators. We gladly substitute society's props for what lies within—free of charge, authentic, multidimensional, and rich in meaning and purpose. Prairie dwellers can find themselves in the midst of a different reality, however.

Things are not as abundant on the grasslands, nor do most things take center stage even when available. There is a natural cautiousness on the prairie, a desire to honor what is real, what is tested and true. As a carryover from the pioneer era, many trust hardship more than materialistic distractions of any brand or variety; most respect and trust the strength of their surroundings and heritage to the point where man-made objects, no matter how magnificent, no matter how impressive, have a tough time competing for their attention and loyal affection.

When there is love in your heart—of the land, of nature, of family and friends—external objects, while they can be a genuine source of inspiration and pleasure, don't take on undue meaning; they don't become cheap and senseless substitutes for what is real. On the prairie lands I grew up with, there is a quiet, but noticeable, sense of purpose. It comforts many—acting as an invisible buffer, a silent protector—against the onslaught of media and hype dished out by a seemingly sophisticated, twenty-first-century world.

And from this quiet-sense-of-purpose perspective springs an intuitive understanding of pretentious ways that alienate and divide, keeping people at odds and far removed from one another, and from themselves, by cutting them off from their innermost needs. From what their hearts are frantically trying to tell them.

Yet, this lack of pretense is often misunderstood.

Mistaken for dullness or a lack of distinction, sometimes perceived as naiveté or taken to suggest a lack of intelligence or formal education, residents are subjected to a variety of derogatory and generally incorrect assumptions about who and what they are. But most take it all in stride, knowing surface impressions never reveal the truth of any matter. They also understand that pleasing themselves, indeed, *being themselves*, generates a quiet sort of confidence, a hopeful outlook, a centered and balanced perspective.

Like the well-built foundation of an exquisite physical structure, these people, especially those who have resided here for some time, are rock solid where it counts, so jeers—silent, spoken, deserved, or undeserved—from the "outside world" hold little power over them. Comfortable with a lifestyle that literally "sprung from the prairie," the people I grew up around adorned themselves in basic fashions (most out-of-date regardless of income); they drove old cars or pickups for the most part; they lived in modest homes, prepared simple, but healthy food; they went to movies on a seldom, don't-have-to-see-it-right-now basis; they took plenty of walks in the evening, stopping to chat with neighbors and friends; they routinely helped people in need; they talked to each other on a regular basis; they enjoyed nature, outdoor activities, whenever possible. *They kept it simple.*

Sometimes because they had to, sometimes because they wanted to, but always because they valued what they had, even if the world beyond, trapped in elements of make-believe, didn't quite understand. Outsiders, sometimes caught up in the external elements of life (the glittery gift wrap, for example), may not realize that prairie dwellers insist on opening the box before appraising the contents. A natural way of life for many, such people aren't easily fooled by the artificial, the expensive, or the ornate.

Mark Peterson, a Lutheran pastor living in Buffalo, wrote about the "Wide Open Space" for *South Dakota Magazine.* He expresses a growing appreciation for what is actually here, even if it appears to be "less than" by those who may not fully appreciate life with the land.

Occasionally the mid-morning sun is obscured by a racing cloud and my squinting eyes can open to take in more fully the expanse that surrounds me. I can see to the horizon maybe 50 miles away. Brown grass is bent over and bobbing like a rushing river on both sides of me. . . . Such wide open space surrounds me and the wind, the breath of the prairie herself grabs at me and pushes my car. . . . It is overbearing. As a city boy, transplanted here not more than a few years ago, I found it a difficult transition. So much sky, so vast a prairie, such force of wind. There is no escape. . . . This prairie knows me; there is no way to escape her relentless gaze. . . . Living under her daily gaze has left me with no alternative. There is communion. I have come to find that there is an unspoken bond between this wind, this landscape, and those who live here constantly surrounded in her relentless grasp. A trinity, one might say. Though I try without success to maintain some sort of distance, it is a futile effort. . . . These wide open spaces rip open my soul. She can see deep within. She knows who I am and where I am going, perhaps better than myself. This can be intimidating—being known in such a way. . . . As I look back, I now know that my several months of anxiety upon arrival to this area was a result of this prairie herself. Her deep blue eyes, her brown etched skin sinking deeply into my being. . . . Though I still try to hide, it comes as a difficult realization that I will endlessly be known by her.

We are all weathering some kind of storm—literal, figurative, ongoing or sudden and then gradually dissipating. But maintaining a quiet sense of purpose can steady us, calm us, and definitely enlighten us. It's just another prairie truth I learned along the way.

Legend has it that Jesse James jumped across a wide and deadly chasm in the rocks near Garretson, South Dakota, while evading pursuers. The chasm is called Devil's Gulch. . . . Devil's Gulch is one of those unlikely features on the prairie. It shows up with great suddenness.

~WAYNE FANEBUST,
Tales of Dakota Territory,
Volume I

CHAPTER SEVEN
Noticeable Vibrancy

FREEDOM: A STRONG STATEMENT, an envied condition by many, a word that rings with emotion and choice, an elusive goal, a fantasy perhaps. As a whole, we are a people who admire staying power and commitment as much as we relish the idea of being free to follow our heart's desire; thus, we are forced to play a tough balancing act between our dependent and independent sides. Often enough, we are unsuccessful in our attempt to find peace and harmony within this challenging, ever-shifting context.

I'm reminded of the married couple trying to accommodate each other's need for freedom, at least in some measure, while at the same moment wanting to stay close. Love can be a confusing, sometimes overpowering emotion, causing us to wonder and worry about its very expression, its motives and purposes. The prairie lands are a reflection

Always Returning

of this dichotomy—confining while simultaneously offering a sense of unabridged freedom. As one longtime resident explained: there is something about prairie life that fosters a sense of independence; there is always a desire to see what is over the next hill. These same lands, when lodged in your heart and soul, also hold you in place—making their place known and felt in lasting ways.

I know this feeling well.

I'm always returning—physically, mentally, spiritually—to the deep and abiding sense of place I grew up with. It seems I'm in good company. Listen to these prairie-wise voices from essays appearing in *Leaning into the Wind, Women Write from the Heart of the West:*

> *And you have to understand that I love this place. It is my home. I am free and bound. If that sounds a dichotomy, you have not caught the proper balance; I could not be secure if I were not allowed freedom. I have to have room to think and to call upon the strength I take from solitude. I have to run to the hills and look into the sweep of prairie and the river and the distance and I have to leave here and I have to come back.*
> —JOAN HOFFMAN, "HOME ON THE RANGE"

> *We still stand under the stars and talk about faith and loss and dreams, and we are still teenage Western girls who grew up free.*
> —KAREN OBRIGEWITCH, "GROWING UP FREE"

Noticeable Vibrancy

The prairie is in me like the dirt is in the earth—or in the mulberries.
—BERNIE KOLLER, "MULBERRIES"

I love the land so much I feel joined to it. As you walk over the prairies and hills, walk softly, for you tread on my soul. . . . This is my history and future, the wind blows so fierce it might blow through my veins.
—PATTY LITZEL, "GIFTS FROM THE SKY"

Do you hear the deep emotions running through these words—sense the love expressed for a place sometimes discounted as empty, barren? Notice the fierce independence running through the souls of these women despite and because of their deep connection to the land? Put your ear to the ground. *Listen.*

Stake a Claim

During the spring and summer months wild prairie flowers are eager to stake a claim on the land. Almost like a sudden gift of fate, they appear in random order, scattered here and there as if someone dropped a basket of seed for the wind to scatter with considerable abandon. A pleasing palette of colors, shapes, and sizes quickly intensifies, dotting the resting landscape with everything from petite-looking Pasque flowers (the state flower, and also called prairie smoke or the May Day flower, is bell-shaped, lavender, and belongs to the buttercup family) in early spring to yellow star grass and daisies of all varieties in the summer. As the ground warms, the prairie scene radiates a noticeable vibrancy.

As if anxious to make their mark, prairie flowers sometimes surprise visitors with their determined presence amid the free-flowing grasses. Even during the intense heat of summer, with long dry spells and backbreaking wind that blows like it will never, never stop, the native flowers march on. Merely built into the prairie's mystique, the tiny, timid flowers of spring (our Pasque flower often emerges before the last snow can clear the ground) gradually give way to tall, sturdy-looking varieties in yellow, gold, and purple that blend with the native grasses as if an artist's brush had graced a massive outdoor set with incredible imagination. With indescribable passion.

The wildflowers contribute to the feeling of freedom that floats through the air like fluffy white cotton from stately cottonwood trees. Truly intoxicating, there is nothing contrived or pretentious about a determined show of color blending in, almost unnoticeably at times, with a scene straight from *Little House on the Prairie* by Laura Ingalls Wilder.

Simultaneously, the native flowers seem to proclaim, "I am here to stay. This is where I belong. This land is part of me. I will *never* leave." As if they have effectively staked their claim, like the pioneers and settlers of old, these colorful gems—snow white and sunshine yellow—know their place; they know the value of staying close to the land.

Like the people who inhabit this area, these flowers, smallish or showy or somewhere in between, offer us insight and inspiration. Being a survivor has its rewards and pluses; being a pleasant contrast to the not-so-pleasant side of life can be joyful and exhilarating; being lovely and beautiful and uplifting is worthwhile; being low in maintenance can be perfect. Being natural and carefree—well, what could be better?

Follow Your Heart
What, I wonder, was tucked in the heart of hearts of a settler back in the mid-to-late 1800s? Sure, we have read our history books—we know what we think we know—but do we really know the heart and soul of the average pioneer? Reluctant or enthused? Frozen with fear or moving forward with hope, courage, commitment?

There are those who believe the great majority of settlers headed west out of economic necessity; that they also hated the uncertainty, danger, and daily strife of trying to survive on the unsettled, barren-looking prairie lands offering the seldom tree, a rare rain shower, a desert-type sun, a merciless wind, and in the winter, blinding snow sent down from above to freeze and punish living creatures. A place created to intimidate the few brave souls daring to venture forth into the prairie's daunting sphere.

Yet something tells me there had to be more. People who want to climb Mount Everest, who set their sights on professional baseball, who take on steep challenges of all varieties, have something in common: a passion for the task ahead, a deep love for whatever has captured their heart, a burning desire to push themselves beyond normal endurance levels—to test their strength and ability and commitment.

It seems that a good number of the settlers must have felt like this, otherwise, how could they have prevailed when the deck was obviously stacked in favor of nature, the land, the trying conditions? It seems incomprehensible to me to write off their often heroic efforts as an economic necessity. And it feels like a disservice of incredible magnitude to downplay their innumerable accomplishments—amazing, admirable, absolute—for any reason, really.

Regardless of why, irrespective of the tangled motivations that came into play, we need to remember and honor their journey into the unknown. By discounting what they endured to make new lives for themselves, we only grow more cynical, more disenchanted. Viewed in a more realistic light, it's safe to say that the pioneer spirit, a desire to strike out on one's own despite the odds and inevitable hardship, is worth emulating. It's worth rekindling such genuine desire in our hearts. Even though this may be impossible to always accomplish in a geographical sense, emotionally, spiritually, and intellectually, it's entirely feasible.

The plethora of complex issues facing our global society are seriously challenging, if not more so than during prior times in our history. Yet they have to be faced. To do otherwise is to shrink from life out of fear, to become less with each passing generation.

Who will our children be inspired by, if not by us? What will our country become if we stop reaching for the stars, forget to dig deeper for the very essence of life—the rich core from which wondrous truths derive?

What are we waiting for, I wonder. And why are we so captivated, so entirely taken in by violence; it seems to show up everywhere, as a "normal" life component. In movies, books, homes, schools, and playgrounds. For me, it's a mystery of immense proportions. When life *can* be grand and beautiful, we choose to make it less; we denigrate our very existence with senseless, hateful acts reflecting our discontent like the most accurate thermometer in the universe. Like robots without hearts, souls, or minds, we seem unable to stop, incapable of changing our direction, even while the rewards are invisible, the damage all too visible. And no matter what parents do as caring, deeply concerned individuals, society and peer groups (culture) are the paramount influences to be reckoned with. A dysfunctional group mentality and collective influence are powerful forces that lack accountability of any kind.

Kindred Spirits
Again, we look to the prairie—the place and its people—for hints and, yes, for wisdom. When asked "What makes Dakota special?" one person replied: "The people, the majority of South Dakotans have an innate kindness." Perhaps it's because they aren't far removed from their pioneer ancestry.

It's true.

A sense of struggle, and therefore compassion, lingers in the sweet-smelling prairie air like a stubborn soldier of old—one who refuses to be stamped out by time or experience. And since nature reigns supreme, the people watch, with a skeptical eye, anyone who tries to rise above the mystical forces governing the land, their way of life. Their ways are tried, tested, and true; they are trusted, revered, and loved. You can hear it in their voices, feel it in their warmth, see it in their actions. They haven't forgotten the wisdom of the old ways. They see merit in striking out on their own; value in staking a claim—no matter how small or seemingly insignificant.

For one thing, it's a way to deal with the uncertainty of existence.

Instead of sinking into a do-nothing mind-set, a victim mentality, many of these people, in a carryover from the past, still like to make their own mark on the world. In grandiose proportions, probably not. Of meritorious ramifications, possibly.

You see, this can-do spirit keeps us charged with enthusiasm for life, ready and willing to take on the next challenge. As if we've learned to thrive on adversity, when things go awry, we tend to pick ourselves up, dust ourselves off: push on. As one gentleman said: "Can't stand to be burnin' daylight."

Our pioneer woman, Frances Nickel Jones shared this incredible story.

> *Back in 1923, I became ill when we lived in the log house. I was taken to the hospital; I had pneumonia*

> *in both lungs. I was in the hospital more than four months, flat on my back in bed for more than three of those months. Two or three times, I was not expected to live. My boys were six and eight years old. I worried about them constantly for fear they would be bitten by a rattlesnake or harmed by some accident. Yet I could not see them or do anything to help. They only got to town to see me one time. My husband was so busy trying to take care of the ranch work, the boys had to take care of themselves most of the time. I prayed day and night to God to take care of my boys and to help me get well so I could go home and take care of them and help with other things.*

But Frances goes on to point out that her sons were "good boys," that the years spent on the prairie were "good years. They taught me many things I would never have known, like patience and trying to help others in any way I can."

She lights the way for those who are timid or fearful of encountering difficult times. Her charm, confidence, and emotional strength speak volumes about the value of knowing who you are and where you are going. Like an invisible anchor, this pioneer woman's ability to keep fighting back probably saved her life a few times. And she, like many other kindred spirits, helps preserve the endearing prairie spirit—even when the value of striking out on one's own is minimized in favor of the safe course, the path of minimal resistance.

Unlike the sturdy prairie flowers, some have forgotten the importance of valor, and even though many of us have the pluck to think and act independently, even when risky or ill-advised, how often do we exercise such options?

How often do we follow our hearts into the wilderness of our souls—into the vast unknown of our ever so unique internal landscapes?

Surely as vast as the prairie itself, as the high-powered Dakota sky, if not more so, we shun our interior worlds in exchange for showy exteriors made of disposable products. A safer route, of course; an easier reality, most assuredly; a less confounding perspective from which to view life, from which to puzzle our way through, certainly. Yet we miss so much. Like turning our back on a splendid sunset, strolling through a lovely summer garden with our eyes shut tight, or entering a bakery with a gunnysack over our head, we close ourselves off to the best life has to offer.

Robert Adams, a retired astronomer (article published by *South Dakota Magazine*), offers this: "Fortunately, here in South Dakota . . . we may still enjoy such things as the subtle colors of dusk where the marriage of light and darkness produce the offspring of quiet beauty and peace." He goes on: "In few places does the universe open its arms to the sensitive observer in such welcome."

Noticeable Vibrancy

Yet how often do we fail to notice, to look, with all our senses tuned in, to the stunning beauty that beckons overhead and within? The remedy: Choose a path requiring courage and heart; strike out on your own. It will open your eyes—to life, and to yourself.

I've taken my fun where I've found it.
~RUDYARD KIPLING,
"The Ladies"

CHAPTER EIGHT
A Sense of Poetry

DO YOU EVER THINK ABOUT the role of fun in your life? Do you squeeze it in around the edges like the last-minute cuff link, the almost forgotten birthday card to Aunt Sally, the hurried phone call to a distant friend? Or is it the frosting on the cake, the best part? Even then, do you ever feel guilty consuming "all that frosting," knowing you are eating the piece of cake mostly because of the sugary, sweet layer (in your favorite flavor) on top?

These questions, rhetorical to be sure, only set the stage for a look at life, scanning for fun—for bits and pieces of time spent enjoying the moment, relishing the activity or the companionship that makes you smile, relax, or simply feel happy. Because it seems, as I consider the lifestyles and proclivities of people, institutions, and organizations, that we have come to downplay the importance of building

Always Returning

fun into our twenty-first-century lives. Maybe, on a deeper level, we have forgotten how to have fun.

Consider your priorities for a minute.

Where does fun appear: near the top, or hovering, in a shaky kind of way, at the bottom? Is it there at all? Quite possibly you equate it with something expensive or frivolous, even impossible; maybe fun, to you, is only to be experienced when all of the serious aspects of life have been taken care of first. I've met people who kept a lid on fun for fear it would come to dominate their time. After all, we are taught the importance and considerable merit of responsibility from a young age. We hear this: "Get your work done *first*, then play."

So, naturally, we begin to segregate our lives into work and play, as a lasting tug-of-war emerges; eventually, many of us give up, tossing "fun" aside. Then we rush to justify our choice, if we are even aware of making it, by scornfully considering the lives of others (the minority, to be sure) who seem intent on having fun no matter what. Do we not envy them really? Their curious ability to keep worry, responsibility at bay—at least in perspective—when we have become slaves to our overly serious sides. To the things in life that are *supposed* to bring us happiness.

But do such promises ever deliver to the extent we expect them to, or are we met instead with nameless feelings of discontent?

John Chaffee, Ph.D., author of *The Thinker's Way: 8 Steps to a Richer Life,* comments on the meaninglessness of our age, pointing out that: "We are too busy 'living' to wonder *why* we are living or who is doing the living. But can we afford to be too busy to find meaning in our lives?" he asks, suggesting that: "Our lives depend on the answer to this question. Not our biological lives necessarily, but the life of our *spirit*."

Chaffee quotes theologian Paul Tillich, stressing his belief that we need the "courage to be" to create a life of meaning and purpose that is *individually* significant. Yet how can we create such a life when we ignore the wisdom of old ways, prairie-wise notions of those who still sculpt meaningful lives based on simple, soulful concepts? We've grown so smart, we *think;* we've become so "sophisticated" in our choices; and yes, we believe we've become so unlike those who preceded us.

It's truly uncanny, our ability to deceive ourselves.

Some people have even convinced themselves they don't need fun.

They are too busy, too polished, too broke, too bored by it all, too mature and rational to engage in something our children, our grandchildren, might thrive on. Maybe, at times, we all tell ourselves, like a parent to a child, that we can get by without such silly, time-wasting diversions, because we always must be engaged in a relentless pursuit of whatever the world labels success.

Taken in by our own sense of importance—feelings of infallibility, false confidence—we willingly settle for a meaningless existence over one that offers *life*.

Prairie Fun

Not sure where or when the saying "kick up your heels" came to be, I recall hearing this phrase as a young person growing up in the middle of nowhere. In other words: *Have some fun.* While common to other parts of the country, as well, I associate the old saying with the Wild West, the cowboy era. Cowboy boots have heels, or some such logic.

Fun, in that era, seemed to be built into the culture—almost unnoticeably; fun was the frosting on the cake, but it was also part of the cake itself. As an avid observer of societal trends and transformations, I wonder if we haven't lost touch with our ability to laugh at ourselves, to allow for mistakes and related good humor. Maybe we've forgotten how to build fun into our daily lives, and especially into our work.

With so much pressure to perform—no matter what our occupational status or personal situation—our focus may have narrowed, our hearts and souls may have shriveled from neglect and worry. Consider the national crime rate, increased competition for rewarding careers, parents who cannot get it all done, crowded classrooms with underpaid teachers, students who have tuned it all out, movies and books filled with violence and dissension, shifting or sinking values, a moral maze, misguided priorities, a burgeoning population, an abundance of superficial lifestyles that seem to alienate and divide.

Where is the balance, the joyful dance of laughter between like-minded souls? Where is our ability to interject a sense of poetry into our harried lives? There are exceptions, plenty of them, yet every society has an essence: a core that radiates its most compelling aspects and properties. With the plethora of self-help books on the market, the

A Sense of Poetry

increasing number of "where-have-we-gone-wrong" type programs (TV, radio, private counselors), it's apparent that we feel shaky, uncertain, and disenchanted. Newspaper headlines remind us of this on a very black-and-white level, but more important, we seem to know we've lost our way. Yet we seem unable to help ourselves, to look into our hearts and souls for answers.

Curiously overwhelmed by the enormity of the task, we remain frozen and fearful as we passively wait for something—anything—to impact the status quo in a positive fashion. On the prairie, however, where people somehow keep their sights within mortal limits, it is no wonder that, despite it all—harsh weather, limited economic opportunity, outsiders who callously advocate turning the area into a giant zoo and theme park (Buffalo Commons or some such thing) or maybe a landfill for waste disposal, modest to low income levels per capita, cultural tensions of old, and snide comments from those who look down on residents as somehow less than those who live elsewhere—people just keep on having fun.

Many appear to do this by keeping a healthy and positive sense of perspective, by truly valuing what they have—even when others insist on knocking it—and by not being overly influenced by what goes on around them in terms of global events.

Because, truly, there is always a crisis somewhere.

Consider this insightful commentary by Josh Holland of Tabor. At sixteen, as a junior in high school, Holland was asked to describe the state's strengths and shortcomings for *South Dakota Magazine*. His thoughts are memorable, if not wise.

> *In 1989* Newsweek *depicted South Dakota of the future as a giant zoo and theme park, and as a new frontier for waste disposal. I was a fifth-grader then, intent on putting the magazine in its place as well as any ten-year-old could, so I joined with some friends to write a letter to the editor.* Newsweek *didn't publish it, but the editor sent us a letter of apology. Seven years later, I haven't forgotten that article. Who would dare think of turning this state into a landfill after seeing a Black Hills sunset? How could you turn South Dakota's heritage and tradition into a "Pirates of the Caribbean" experience? Nothing contrived can capture the essence of this place.*
>
> *I think of South Dakota as a stone among stones. It's too easy to think of certain other states as gems. Once California was golden; now many people there think of it as pyrite. To me South Dakota is a geode, plain at first glance, but filled with a multitude of dazzling facets.*

Josh seemed to understand more about life than many; he was able to put his feelings into words that anyone could appreciate; he was able to grasp the significance of the prairie—its timeless value, its inspirational spirit, its nonconforming ways—in a clear, determined manner. You

A Sense of Poetry

have to admire his serious spunk: his ability to defend his home, the place, he obviously loves.

Typical of prairie dwellers, a feisty attitude is indeed a desirable trait; it often conceals a genuine happiness, a knowing heart, a true kindness, a secret.

No matter what others do or say to minimize or reduce the prairie and her people, this confident group will go on doing what they've always done. Unwilling to jump through a myriad of exhausting hoops to please strangers, prairie residents merely try to please themselves. In doing this, many have learned not to take things too seriously.

It would hurt too much, making them bitter and resentful; and it would surely cause them to quit having fun. And even though it may be disguised as hard work—masquerading as an everyday activity built into the day in a seamless, almost invisible, fashion—fun comes in a variety of shapes and sizes on the prairie. Its role, important and life enhancing, hasn't been forgotten or supplanted by executive privilege, nor has *real* fun been replaced by exclusive high-dollar events, expensive products, or artificial definitions. Clearly, it hasn't turned into something that only looks the part.

Sense of Adventure

On remote stretches of land, many people have learned to turn mundane tasks and limited resources into something more. Granted, it takes creativity, a willing heart, and a strong belief in simple, down-to-earth expectations, but having fun is a state of mind as much as anything, something undertaken to nourish the soul, to round out the rough edges life has a way of generating.

Very little is prepackaged on the prairie, however, so fun requires a powerful sense of imagination and adventure. And it may require true respect for the healing power of humor, general goodwill, and the emotional bonding that derives from sharing laughter with others. From the low-key picnic to the Sunday drive in the country, or maybe it's the high school rodeo, hunting prairie dogs, or a potluck wedding shower, fun is truly what you make it on the prairie. And even though these people often work long, hard days—especially farmers and ranchers—that doesn't mean there is no time for fun. Rather, they simply build it into the project of the day whether that means branding cattle, putting up hay, harvesting wheat, canning pickled beets, planting a garden, or heading to an office for the day.

Even if it means taking time at lunch to throw a few horseshoes, play a hand of poker, or linger for a few jokes when the workday is over, there isn't much room for disappointment because expectations are blissfully realistic. Here's what prairie experts shared:

"Fun to me is not what a lot of other folks would call fun. I like to see something gained—to me, that is fun. To be friendly and have friends, and any work activity that turned out well."

"Fun is anything that makes me laugh. When the people one works with take the time to laugh and joke about things, any work activity becomes enjoyable."

A Sense of Poetry

"Fun is work that you enjoy."

A carryover from the days of the settlers, perhaps, this idea that fun doesn't have to be neatly segregated from work or ignored in the pursuit of loftier goals is captured here by Laura Ingalls Wilder: "The American pioneer spirit (is) of courage, jollity, and neighborly helpfulness."

So when you get a chance to visit the prairie, leave your fancy duds behind; you won't need them at all, nor will you need to wait in a long line to buy a ticket to a sophisticated musical production. You won't need to plan too far in advance, either, but you may want to bring your camera. Nature walks are on the prairie menu, along with looking skyward to catch stirring sunsets that burn in your memory like a first kiss. Fishing may very well be in order, or making jelly with a neighbor, or maybe a church group is forming a softball team; and sometimes the best fun of all is casual, unplanned conversation—the weather, the crops, the kids, the politics of the day, the tall newcomer from out East, the passing of a longtime friend, the birth of a child. As long as there are people and prairie, opportunities for fun will exist because *real* fun dwells in the heart and soul just waiting for an excuse to show itself.

Everything an Indian does is in a circle, and that is because the power of the world always works in circles, and everything tries to be round.

~JOHN G. NEIHARDT,
Black Elk Speaks, Being the Life Story of a Holy Man of the Ogalala Sioux

CHAPTER NINE

In a Circle

I T NEVER CEASES TO AMAZE ME. We know nothing happens in isolation, that the world has a rhythm, a rhyme, of its very own, that everything is somehow connected, yet, without fail, we squirm against this reality like a new puppy on its first leash. We want to believe in our omnipotence, to conceal our natural and undeniable vulnerability; most assuredly, we want to downplay the significance of forces we cannot see or fully understand.

But don't we set ourselves up, albeit knowingly, willingly?

By straining to move in opposition to a fundamental and universal law, we usually make things more difficult. Going against the grain, the natural intent or direction, can drum up an underlying friction. While this can generate a positive force, something to stimulate change, more often, our reluctance to acknowledge the interdependence of all living creatures—the unpredictable intertwining of events and unexplained happenings—contributes to our stress level, adds to our frustration. We spin our wheels, wondering why so little progress is made. Worse yet, we exert precious energy and waste time blaming politicians, the media, and the weather in an effort to "isolate" and define problems.

Never bothering to examine the interrelationship between situations, circumstances, and people, we sometimes ignore commonsense solutions in favor of a need to arbitrarily segregate good and bad, known and foreign, popular and unpopular—all because we don't like complexity (or maybe because we've never questioned what we absorbed as children). As a society, we seem to gravitate toward finger pointing and easy explanations requiring little of us on an emotional, spiritual, or intellectual level.

Have we lost our ability to try, to look for win-win solutions, to address critical problems from a fresh and novel perspective? In many contexts, we've simply given up, are no longer looking for a better way. But where is our pioneer spirit, our courage, our willingness to *try*? Growing up with the prairie, I experienced a constant visual reminder of the omnipotence of nature—grasses swaying back and forth like a silent metronome; an expansive sky that welcomes, protects, inspires, and sometimes explodes; nighttime stars dotting the black heavens like a infinite sea of diamonds; wide-open ranges—shortgrass to tallgrass to mixed—needing nothing more than air, soil, and water to make their mark—and something seemed to nudge me to view things differently.

With compassion and a steadfast aura, the magnanimous prairie spirit suggested a path with greater dignity and grace: one to encompass instead of exclude, one to unite instead of tearing apart, one to appreciate the connectedness of people and place and time, not just the inevitable disparities. It seemed that I'd been put in my place then and forever more. My life wasn't a meaningless string of random events to juggle, to divide and arrange at will, but a reflection of something greater—something connected to a much grander stage harboring cosmic dimensions.

The prairie had also called to my attention the vastness of nature—bigger, broader than any individual—with a compelling panoramic view; it fostered a vantage point that included everyone and everything without picking, choosing on an arbitrary basis. Definitely freeing, this sort of perspective encouraged me to appreciate the very human qualities in people while not expecting perfection, artificial distinctions, or endless comparisons (too often ugly, unfair, and needless) that seemed to make the world go round.

For one thing, it felt unkind; for another, it seemed mildly destructive. And finally, such "me against you" orientations seemed unsophisticated and self-indulgent; negative, unholy, and certainly careless. Human beings needn't be judged so harshly, quite so swiftly. Why are we so eager to pass judgment on others, on their intentions, as if we, mere mortals, are godlike? Aren't we in this together—this thing called life—and if any aspect of our earthly experience can be improved, aren't we all better off, really?

These were some of my thoughts growing up prairie-wise in the fifties, sixties, and early seventies; while I eagerly posed more questions than ever could be fully answered, many of my deepest convictions grew from my early meanderings. And even though I chose to stray from my prairie roots during my adult years—always returning, of course—I've continued to ponder life deeply, only to grow somewhat circumspect about voicing ideas that might be labeled idealistic, or quickly rebuffed because they dare to question mainstream viewpoints. Unfortunately, though, the trending opinion of the day is rarely the wisest perspective.

Connect the Dots

Still, to this day I envision a world where people recognize the importance of multiple roles, of working harmoniously together to create a marvelous whole, where mending fences and caring about relationships is more important than burning bridges. And since the most basic picture isn't complete until all the pieces connect, until the image takes shape as a whole, there is a certain amount of prairie wisdom in exploring the big picture while we still have an opportunity to have a significant impact. Life and death inevitably come full circle, too, or like a genuine cowboy might say: "We're all gonna kick the bucket."

In a Circle

This topic isn't mentioned to be morbid or overly somber; nor is it a prairie pastime to spend an inordinate amount of time thinking about death. Rather, to better understand the circular design of the world, to live and work and love within a framework of mystical yet predictable design, there is value in examining the final, culminating event from a wiser perspective. Among the people—and remember, this isn't a culture marked by youth, fancy cars, expensive clothes, flashing neon lights, fads or superficial lifestyles—death is part of life. Not in a detached, wringing-of-the-hands sense; rather, death exists in a pure context of ultimate surrender to the land. By inviting quiet contemplation concerning the truths of our existence, the profound mystery of life and death, we grow closer to universal rhythms.

Formed of the past and sustained by the present, the prairie culture I *know* is rich, warm, and real. Without pretense, undue complication, or weighty expectations, unadorned beauty seems to be the underlying theme. To those who notice the unspoken, it feels refreshing and powerful, yet peaceful and invigorating, inspiring and utterly distinctive.

To me, the prairie and its people, radiate completeness, and in seeking nothing more, in an openness to being a place of natural dimensions, the enduring land—without fanfare or sharp comment—also resembles a final resting place. While linked to beginnings of remarkable stride, while supporting growth and longevity, simultaneously, the prairie invites its inhabitants to sleep peacefully when the last breath is taken.

Always Returning

Come home, day is done. *Come home.*

When I really listen—stand still, look and breathe with full awareness—it's almost like hearing a faint heartbeat. The heartbeat of the cosmos.

Circle of Life

What part of the universal circle does your life, indeed, your soul, represent; what aspects of your immediate circle does your heart wrap itself around—protectingly, lovingly, and joyfully? In fact, how many circles does your life impact on; are they distant, of moderate proximity, close or intimate?

Maybe you have never thought about your life in such terms.

But in the end, it is the circle of life that draws us close, keeping us focused on what is meaningful. On what is truly true.

Envision a circle of life-sustaining covered wagons, white, but dust covered and almost touching: one to one, in a snug, tightly held ring. A shield against the forces that be, seen and unseen; a symbol of unity; a perfect reflection of the pioneer spirit; a source of power, love, and fortitude—all of this marked the appearance of wagon trains at rest in a traditional circle at nightfall when the prairie grew dark, mysterious, seemingly endless.

Have things changed substantially since the mid-to-late 1800s—since the era of covered wagons and creaking wooden wheels rolled steadily across rough ground in a valiant search for opportunity and freedom: for an inspirational domain offering new life?

In a Circle

Most people, still and possibly forever more, are in search of something they don't quite understand. At night, when cool breezes filter in around the campfire, when the heavens turn dark yet splendid with an actual peek into infinity, we gather our circle of friends and loved ones together, for warmth and protection and inspiration as we reflect on the day, restoring our spirits for the days yet to come, as we faithfully wait for the dawn.

For a poetic description of the prairie's incredible power—how it can provoke, subdue, and overwhelm, encouraging us to draw close against the night—I recommend the words of author O.E. Rölvaag in his opening chapter, "Toward the Sunset," from *Giants in the Earth*, first published in 1927.

Knowledge Comes, Wisdom Lingers

Another circular construct bearing meaning and dignity for nearly everyone—treasured family relationships, especially those between young and old. From Singapore to Alaska to the prairie lands, their unique configurations buoy our lives in innumerable ways. I recall my grandmother's old age with a mixture of sadness and joy: a wonderful human being, a work of art, a personal treasure beyond anything I'd ever known. Yet I knew she wouldn't be with us forever; she knew it, too.

Looking back, I wonder if we were truly sensitive to that reality, or did we dance around the inevitable out of a basic discomfort with our emotions; did we fail to honor the fear, the impending sense of loss and finality, that had quietly wrapped itself around our interactions with her?

Always Returning

Like a brilliant moon in a darkened sky, the light of her soul captured our hearts, touched our souls with something nameless, almost primitive, yet we seemed to lack the courage (or the spiritual awareness) to say: "Thank you." For all she had done, for all she had given us, for her knowledge, her considerable wisdom, for showing us how to live, for teaching us the importance of truth, kindness, and concern. Yes, we told her of our love; we hugged her and smiled; she smiled back, then winked—even into her nineties—as if she'd happily shared a tantalizing secret with us. A woman of the prairie, having lived a long life without luxuries, fanfare, or pretense, having never driven an automobile, she radiated a sense of perfection, peace, and utter completeness; it should have prompted us to thank her for sharing her life with us, simple words with such incredible power.

I guess we thought she knew, or maybe we didn't stop to think about the obvious, about how much those words might have meant to her. Yet saying thank you is such a wonderful acknowledgment of another person's role in your life—your success, your defeats and hard times, your joys. Two incredible words that sum up the circular nature of relationships and life, they indicate respect, caring, appreciation, and, ultimately, equality, understanding, and empathy. What could be more important—almost like a celebration of life itself—to say to a person you've loved deeply, someone you've quietly appreciated since you were old enough to smile, someone facing the end of life as we know it?

In a Circle

Very little. But we shy away from it in this context because those everyday words force us to come to terms with reality: A loved one is about to complete his or her circle of life. Painful, yes, so we make small talk to avoid talking about the things that matter, the things we need and want to say. *We chicken out.* Yet I look at the personal story of Frances Nickel Jones, the courageous prairie woman introduced earlier, and at 104, she begins eight pages of handwritten notes like this: "Dear Friend Daisy, Thank you for this opportunity to help you, if I can with your book—I do wish you success."

Then she goes on to tell me about her years in a log house on the prairie in the early 1900s: that she was born in Illinois in 1895, that her mother died in 1905, and that her father, feeling unable to care for the three children, placed them in separate foster homes. The family she was placed with moved to South Dakota in 1909. Meanwhile, her father married again: "He and his wife had seven more children. I am the oldest of all of the ten children—and today I am the only one of the ten children left. I guess South Dakota has been a good place for me to live." Frances recalls being at her mother's bedside as a young girl (ten years old) when she died: "That was a hard thing for me to do—then I lost my first baby boy during childbirth—then in 1928 I lost my first husband because of a stroke. I lost my second husband in 1972. During these years I lost my brother and my seven half-sisters and brothers. I lost my oldest son, Louie, in 1995. He had cancer. In 1997 I lost my ninety-five-year-old sister. The hardest of all of these to part with was my son—I still miss him so much—he was so good to me. It is hard for a mother to give up her children."

She closes with this heartfelt message: "If you can get any help from this letter or the answers to your questions, then I'm glad—With love, Frances Nickel Jones."

To honor her wonderful, life-giving spirit, I want to say: *Thank you*, Frances, for sharing your insights with us in this fearless book of prairie wisdom.

Most of us won't endure what she has; most of us won't reach 104; and most of us won't develop such a humble and knowing heart, one filled with love—with such sincere regard for others. As a source of inspiration, as a vision of what we are all capable of in our finer, more understanding and humane moments, may her lovely spirit, her graceful walk through life guide us in our search for a better road map to the heart.

For the power of the heart should never be underestimated. Few compasses guide us more accurately to the places, beliefs, and people who matter, to the practices and values that keep our world safe and hospitable for all living creatures, to the connections that help us sustain the ever important, indeed glorious, circle of life.

The Power of Home

Statistics reveal the extent to which people move around these days—to a new city, a new country, a new home within the same community. Opportunities for change abound. Living our lives "away from home," as many do, however, has created pockets of discontent within society, mere

In a Circle

fragments of circles dotting the landscape. I sense, at times, a wistful quality to our world that is apparent in people's voices, faces, and dreams—acknowledged and vice versa. "Something is missing" floats in the air, eerily mingling with crowds, hovering just beyond our consciousness like an especially poignant memory, one we can't seem to forget.

Clearly, I can't speak for everyone but, for me, the missing piece (when I felt like this) was home: my place of birth and growing-up years. The prairie. Cut off from my roots for too long, I feel incomplete, melancholy, and though writing about my homeland has been most enjoyable, sharing it with people the world over—a tremendous honor—it's not the same as gazing out at the prairie, or its sky. I doubt I'm unique in this regard, because I know people who also live away from their physical roots, and it's nearly always a mixed blessing leaving incomplete circles floating here and there—leaving our hearts wide open, searching for meaningful connections to replace the ones we have lost.

It reminds me of what I read in a tiny book about the practice of Zen, wherein Charlotte Joko Beck suggests that if she were to scratch the surface of any one person she would find anxiety, fear, pain running amok. And since each of us comprise the world, in the collective sense, imagine the totality of those feelings on the psyche of the world, on us.

The undercurrent of anything can be very strong indeed.

If a portion of your internal pain stems from a feeling of being disconnected from your roots: go home. Share your childhood memories with friends, your children, grandchildren. Close the circle, make it complete, whenever possible. Whether for a short vacation or for more extended stays, there is no clearer reference point for who we are and what we are all about than the home of childhood. As Black Elk suggests in this chapter's opening quote, power always works in circles. Also true of personal power, time spent close to your roots can help you reclaim your sense of personal power, inspiring you onward, lighting your way for the journey that remains with renewed strength, energy, and focus.

And maybe this is a bigger deal for me than for some of you reading this chapter; maybe the place—the Missouri River, the countryside, the artistic blanket of sky, the play of light on nature and wildlife—I call home weaved its way into my soul in unusually lasting ways. Perhaps, as you've journeyed through life, you've truly gone beyond your physical roots—transcended them, so to speak. But something in you is searching for expression; what circle in your life needs attention? A slight repair, perhaps?

I had to wonder why, in the middle of the South Dakota prairie,
Who in their right mind would start a damn dairy.
~BARRY TYLER,
"In Loving Memory of A. B. (Bud) Tyler, 1999"

CHAPTER TEN
Embrace the Past

GOOD, BAD, OR IN-BETWEEN, the past—your past, my past, *our* past—informs the present and the future. Yet evidence of what came before us can seem overshadowed by the pressures, pains, and pleasures of the moment. So it is that we can easily fail to embrace the past: that which instructs, supports, reveals, and prepares us for today, for tomorrow. Fortunately, the force of history is insistent.

The past seeks to be duly recognized and understood, and even when it seems to all but shout at us, we often turn away—too eagerly, too energetically. Are we afraid of what the past represents, of what there is to know, to consider and contemplate? Or does bringing the past into our lives in a meaningful way make us feel unsuitably dressed, like attending a formal event in all the wrong clothes, or like walking in late, just as everyone is leaving?

Always Returning

Nobody wants to feel out of step with the times, nor do we want to feel stuck in the past, forced to watch the rest of the world go by. As the lyrics to a song go, "Your life is now." But what happens, with amazing predictability, when we attempt to ignore something or someone? Something important, relevant, and perhaps meant to be; someone who wants, needs, and depends on our attention, affection, and interest?

Whatever or whoever usually becomes increasingly insistent and impatient, oddly loud, and strangely constant, until we acknowledge the person, place, or thing calling out to us: *until we pay attention.* As some might say, until we stop to smell the roses. On a friend of mine's T-shirt, a favorite, is this: "Climb More Mountains; Read More Books; Eat More Ice Cream; Pick More Daisies." The point is simply to do more of what matters.

The choice is always ours—to actually do the things we frequently ignore or postpone or barely notice. Do these questionable excuses sound familiar? It's just too far away, too long ago, too much bother, too weird, too difficult, too obvious, too impractical, too much work, too expensive, too confusing, or definitely too time-consuming.

If something from your past is bothering you, give in: Go exploring, see what is there. Pulled in one direction or another, usually for a reason, it can be tempting to overlook the past in our mad rush to go (run?) forward, even more tempting to minimize the importance of understanding, accepting, and embracing the past with its imperfections and missteps. Yet its force is real; it pulses through your

Embrace the Past

heart and soul with a life of its own. And by making it yours, instead of ignoring it, discrediting it, you can bring things into a better balance, and find perspective. Then the past no longer holds such great power over you—your present, your future.

In turning to face the past, we discover how much we've changed, grown, and quietly become *more* than yesterday. By comparing our former self with who we are now, it's also possible to appreciate our evolving identity with a certain amount of satisfaction.

It can be truly eye-opening.

On the Dakota prairie the past feels as vital as the present, and the lessons of old are oh-so-clear via weathered barns, country churches, historical markers at every turn, and mature cottonwoods. Even meadowlarks, which don't compete with anything but stretches of graceful, ever present prairie and sky, announce their survival, indeed, their prominence, with an air of timelessness. In bright contrast, we are encouraged to consider our own brief existence, that we have a finite length of time in which to fulfill our dreams. To share, learn, and grow; to fall down and pick ourselves up again, letting our hearts experience: the depths of despair, the beauty and rapture of relationships only a divine power could envisage, the perfect peace of a starlit prairie sky.

And so we are met with a choice: to let our lives slip through our fingers like a ghostly image of short, unknown duration, or to listen to the prairie wind, to its wise counsel, by embracing life in its many dimensions—past, present, future—while we are here.

Since the prairie, or prairies, call to mind an infinite vantage point, the implicit message is one of precision: Amid priceless simplicity, an unchanging, unwavering ability to inspire and involve and encourage even the dreariest, most despondent inhabitant, the prairie can remind us through its mere presence, its spirit, that life isn't something to be taken lightly, or worse yet, for granted. In fact, our connection to a universal purpose is clear when living or standing within the prairie's sphere: a humbling experience that greatly enlarges the idea of roots. More than a family name, a place, or a group of people who comprise your world for many years, having prairie roots means being connected to the past—to eternity?—in a very visible, powerful way. By looking well beyond a single lifetime, beyond what we can see when we glance over our shoulders or down the road, we enlarge our sense of place, and ultimately, our sense of purpose.

Keeping Us Whole
What about our memories, the wondrous role they play in our daily lives? Hardly a day goes by when we don't recall something from our childhood or growing-up years; maybe a few special moments drift into our awareness from out of nowhere. Like the past in action, our remembrances remind us of our strengths, our weaknesses, of all the times when things fell apart or mysteriously came together—when something remarkable made us laugh or cry or simply lose our cool.

Embrace the Past

Memories give us an automatic reference point for situations and people encountered in the present, but they also provide an ongoing guide to the future. Our past, spelled out by the incredible artistry of memories, is an internal library filled with volumes of topics: life and death, relationships, career interests, hobbies, passions, struggle and perseverance, and more. Some memories stand out like they were created yesterday, others fade as though they never happened, and many are blurry. Indistinct. Like straining to see something that's just too far away, the memories are there somewhere, but we can't quite make them out. Some are more like mere sensations with an ephemeral quality, while others seem to dig in, living interminably in our minds without invitation. The sky of our life in a way.

Prairie memories—thoughts, feelings, internal records that locals compile—include the lifelike feel of the land. Indeed, it is the backdrop of their lives, the *living memory* that sets the stage for daily life in all its forms and adaptations. Sometimes it seems that if you look over the next hill, you still might see a sod shanty providing shelter for a pioneer family, a covered wagon, or at least a trail; maybe a small herd of buffalo roaming free.

Or Sitting Bull himself, resting amidst the prairie landscape to consider life and his people. And surely you'll find, scattered about, a few lone campfire rings, extinguished long ago but bearing signs of life—the steady march forward into wide-open lands offering solitude and room to grow.

Always Returning

The past can feel *that real* on a windswept terrain, so it's not uncommon to draw yesterday close to your heart. An ever present force, this great land reminds and focuses: telling us its story each day like a dependable companion, one experienced in matters of the heart, and one that effectively bridges the puzzling gap between past and present and future, fusing them into a splendid whole—a quilt of many colors, an intricate piece of art.

The culture, as a whole, also seems to exemplify the past: slow, reluctant, and seemingly impervious to change. Vivid reminders of bad guys in black hats immortalized for their bad deeds; cowboys and cowgirls gearing up for the next rodeo; nature at the forefront of things.

By design and happenstance, much of it is still here. While this may seem inconsequential, the past can be a rich source of courage, inspiration, and vision. As one person put it after a lifetime of prairie: "The past shows a person that if you have the will to succeed and do a good job, you can overcome most any obstacle."

This comes from someone who had to overcome *many* obstacles. Yet his wiser instincts, his knowledge of self and life and love, led him to believe in the value of experience: Hold it close to your heart, let it linger in a treasured place, *keep it with you—all of this,* unless it damages your sense of compassion or dignity, your heartfelt vision of what you and your life are about. Then it's right to let it go, to move on to new places that offer you peace, joy, and purpose of heart. The past is not meant to hold us captive when its path has grown dim or confining; nor will it hide us from the world for long.

A Shared History

We have an immediate past, along with a more distant past reaching back to our days as an infant; but we also have a built-in past, one that precedes our physical appearance on earth. Ancestors stretching back across the eons, the *personal context* of time, long gone. And we have a shared history in terms of our nation's past. We only directly experience a fraction of our total history, but our lives represent the cumulative effect of time itself, of all that has transpired since the birth of our civilization.

And so it is, at the turn of the century and beyond, that an excellent opportunity arises to consider our nation's past in relation to its present and certainly in terms of its future. More than a history lesson, definitely more than a few snapshots highlighting the highs and lows of an era, when looking through our prairie lens, polished and expertly positioned, we can see so much more.

Time has been a tremendous teacher, one we often underestimate in its legitimate appeal and ability to transform. Powerful, magical, poetic, and inspirational, the passage of time gives us an incredible gift: a second, third, fourth, or fifth chance, and thereby it gives us something even larger, something we seek in differing degrees at various points in our lives—freedom. The freedom to try again, to look again, to grow in understanding.

Always Returning

Somehow apparent from a prairie perspective, our nation's history, indeed, our world's history as reflected in the passage of time reveals, more than anything, a million and one mistakes. But, luckily, we've been granted a seemingly unlimited number of chances to do things differently, from a wiser, more knowing, outlook; and perhaps we've adopted some prairie secrets along the way.

As travelers on a life journey we don't understand—as the past manifested in the present, as pioneers of the twenty-first century—many of us have learned that less is more. And in the context of embracing our nation's past, this realization can be especially illuminating. Some of our bigger mistakes (often on our own soil) seem predicated on a curious need to overpower, to consume and control, to dominate and direct. But muscling our way through every challenging situation—a predictable aggression—isn't always the answer.

Less can be more.

Sometimes we have to let others find their way, because ultimately, we are *all* on a unique learning path, regardless of appearances and assumptions and perceptions.

As our nation's journey takes us into a new millennium with no sign of covered wagons, sod shanties, or one-room schoolhouses dotting the landscape, perhaps our challenge is this: to embrace the past—like it or not, it is our past; to heal the wounds of our time and the eras that preceded us; to celebrate meaningful progress; to take a penetrating look at our world, where it seems to be headed. Then, if you don't sense a path with heart, if you are ill-at-ease with the patterns in your life or with the world direction, or if a nagging little voice is nudging you in different directions—listen. Don't resist trying something new.

But even without our direct intervention, we know nothing stands still for long.

Since the first edition of this book, world and national history have continued to evolve in a multitude of directions. And since determining how the past will continue to influence the present, the future, is largely a guessing game, mistakes will always be a profound facet of reality. *An instructive reality.* But if we nurture a vigorous pioneer spirit, we'll face the myriad challenges that inevitably lie in wait. We'll persist—shun giving up.

*Happiness doesn't depend on what we have
but it does depend on how we feel towards what we have.
We can be happy with little and miserable with much.*

~WILLIAM DEMPSTER HOARD,
American publisher and agriculturist (1836–1918)

CHAPTER ELEVEN
A State of Mind

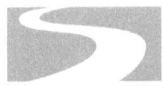

MACHINES, OBJECTS, AND TECHNOLOGY draw reverence from us; human beings with admirable qualities draw mild or passing interest from us, some positive, some negative. Who is he to behave in such a remarkable manner, showing up the rest of us for the whole world to see? Or perhaps our skeptical nature takes over: What is he *really* up to?

While the dynamics of human behavior are rarely clear-cut—some people actually are up to something undesirable—we tend to go out of our way to minimize or negate sentiments and actions that show true merit. When integrity, high standards, compassion, and intelligence make their mark, it exerts a slight pressure on all of us. We wonder if we measure up, and some people even seem to harbor a curious need to sabotage well-meaning efforts.

On a related note, when someone is basically a happy person—supports and encourages others; displays a positive, but realistic, attitude; takes a strong interest in challenges and opportunities without getting bogged down or giving up; presents a warm, caring, and open style: look out. (While an excessive amount of cheerfulness can understandably annoy us, here I'm pointing to a healthy degree of goodness grounded in thoughtfulness, mindfulness, and self-awareness.) Oddly, happy (is contented a better word?) people, often ridiculed or not taken seriously, seem to bug unhappy people to no end.

An entire range of reasons, some legitimate, most nonsensical, come to mind; yet on the prairie, where culture, time, and place join forces to influence our thinking, to shed light on our misconceptions, there is clear evidence of the fundamental value of happiness.

Zero in on your state of mind every now and then. Do you pass on mostly good vibes, a smile, or conversely, do you notice a strange sort of satisfaction, even pleasure, from the trials and tribulations of others—the downside of life? Or maybe you require an excessive amount of external stimulation, an inordinate degree of excitement to feel *happy*.

You believe that life on the prairie, even today, would drive you berserk, causing you to feel bored, unhappy, frustrated, and adrift: someone put out to pasture before his time. And if you are hooked on flashing lights, blaring sirens, fads, trends, new this and that, constant stimulation and superficial novelty—most everything that contributes

A State of Mind

to the sensory overload of the twenty-first century—you may feel especially ill-at-ease with the prairie.

Sensory overload manifests in many ways: time compression (excessively demanding schedules that cause us to feel tense and rushed); an overabundance of material effects; a world economy that neither waits nor rests; a restless, malcontent population; a fast-paced global pulse that dictates many of the terms of everyday life; a quickening of our minds to the point where our hearts and souls can barely keep up.

Of course such trends had a beginning; they aren't entirely new phenomena. Author Robert Hopcke noted in *There Are No Accidents: Synchronicity and the Stories of Our Lives:* "The sad fact of twentieth-century history is, as Einstein remarked, that the development of our technology has outstripped the development of our humanity to the extent that an unparalleled destruction of our human life was made possible in the form of the Holocaust. Not that mass destruction has not always been the shadow of human history...."

Clearly, Dakota, and indeed, our nation, has not been immune to such problems, but if technology was a problem *then*, imagine its effect on our world now. Perhaps in the end, preserving life as we know it will come down to our ability, as a species, to contain the negative effects of a burgeoning technology in relation to our survival.

One thing is certain, and this may seem minor in comparison to some of the issues being addressed, but happy people didn't cause the Holocaust. And while living on a stretch of prairie certainly doesn't guarantee a happy (peaceful?) state of mind, there is, at a minimum, an opportunity to define and discover, from the inside out, what can create and sustain a realistic joy. Quietly forcing us to go beyond conventional, popularized thinking, which spells out and suggests a multitude of ways to "buy" happiness, the prairie, the place and its people, does not advocate specific, one-size-fits-all remedies. Rather, the emphasis, while often understated, can be found in the striking contrast between the outside world and the calm of another world—the prairie's world.

In a place where very little stands between an individual and his or her innermost self, the chances of a genuine encounter are greatly enhanced, and it becomes incumbent on a thinking person to do some soul-searching around the issue of happiness. Contemporary society, with its many bells and whistles, offers a different fare, and while it can create an image of abundance, its impact is faint, more like a mirage.

When genuine happiness—that which endures beyond the moment, in spite of external events and things—is the goal, common sense reminds us of the need for an internal source to replenish our emotions, to sustain a state of mind cultivated and cared for much like a bountiful garden. Otherwise, we're at the complete mercy of what is happening around us and to us, and when it comes to feeling happy, what could be less satisfying, or meaningful?

Happiness can be a choice, something you grant yourself regardless of circumstances; it doesn't have to come

A State of Mind

with a steep price tag as is sometimes assumed. But you have to give yourself permission to be happy despite it all; you have to know how to cultivate a peaceful state of mind. It rarely falls in your lap.

My grandmother, born in 1889, put it this way: "Keep a song in your heart."

And if I were to summarize her approach to life, the timeless guidance she unknowingly left behind through her actions, this is what gave her unlimited joy and happiness, this is what she would have told us at the dawn of the twenty-first century: enjoy nature; tend to your chores; nurture plants, flowers, trees, and animals; appreciate the natural beauty and harvest of life; give away what you don't need; share, smile, laugh, and care; but most of all, keep it simple. So while you must put effort into staying reasonably happy, the road, if filled with heart, isn't as daunting.

Capacity to Learn

The Dakota prairie I grew up with wasn't wont to change its ways. Day after day, month after month, the scene rarely shifted. Sameness ruled. And the prairie stood still for me. For us, as we are born, live, and die. Green and brown grasses, gentle breaks in the land, a wide-eyed sky—a comforting presence suggesting a magnanimous spirit, a happy heart. A living anchor yet a free spirit, one of the prairie's most appealing features. Truly, the land represents both vantage points, an intriguing paradox subject to much interpretation: one of the biggest reasons people literally fall in love with the prairie. Pondering this dichotomy, I realized that the prairie, snow covered or dotted in wildflowers or wearing its plain golden brown of summer and fall, has the power to make me feel happy.

Quite happy, at that.

The prairie represents the perfect state of being (contained, stable, and firmly rooted yet primarily free of manmade influences); it reflects the wholeness of life on a level we will probably never experience. Appealing to our finer senses, it seems to tease and play with our imagination; most important, the prairie, from my perspective, helps us to learn.

In trying to solve its many mysteries, we grow smarter, sometimes wiser.

Most certainly, we grow spiritually.

This kind of soul-searching, dynamic and powerful, can also lead to happiness, because greater self-awareness is often liberating.

Then there is the strong sense of survival the prairie exudes.

Those who live here realize, with a sense of satisfaction, that they are sturdy souls who have adapted and befriended a demanding land, one that challenges through its connection to nature, one that inspires through its natural beauty. But in making peace with the prairie, its power, its starkness, feelings of satisfaction may rise to the surface.

So even as people of the land—insiders, newly arrived outsiders, outsiders on their way to becoming insiders—scurry through their daily routines, the prairie remains steadfast and certain, never wavering or turning away

A State of Mind

yet free to confound and confuse, free to shine on its own terms. And hopefully, we, as a free people, possess the wisdom to preserve, honor, and cherish the open prairie; it offers ample opportunity for self-discovery, and if our humanity is indeed to keep pace with our technology, even in the remotest sense, we will need all the self-awareness we can unearth. Einstein wasn't far off in his assessment of the twentieth century, but let's not continue on that path in a vain attempt to forget the things we already know, in a futile effort to ignore basic human needs, like happiness that is organic, natural, and lasting. Listen to the words of those who love the land; hear the reverence and joy the prairie evokes.

One South Dakota artist, Cherie Ramsdell, who is known for her unique raku pottery (the process was perfected in sixteenth-century Japan) uses her deep connection to the land to further inspire her artistry. When I asked her to describe the most beautiful aspect of prairie life, she offered the following: "To me, it is the ability to be an individual and truly alone for self-reflection. Also the constant reminder that there truly is a force larger than myself. If you question the existence of God all you need to do is lay on an empty prairie, listen, and look up."

Ramsdell also mentions the many things she has learned from prairie life: resiliency, the ability to adapt and innovate, the pure pleasure of hard work and accomplishment.

Mary Jewel Ledbetter, a prairie resident from 1920 to 2012, put it like this when she was 78: "The most beautiful aspect of prairie life is being wrapped around by nature."

She adds: "The prairie teaches patience and perseverance, along with reverence for God's great world—we are part of it all, not masters of it." Finally, Ledbetter said: "I find deep peace when I am looking out over the prairies of western South Dakota. They are closer to heaven than any place on earth. The power of the rolling plains is hard to explain, but easy to feel. The ability to see for forty or fifty miles is exciting—nothing clutters your view!"

Mary Jewel grew up on a sheep ranch and excelled in many different ways. She was also my journalism instructor in high school, a stickler for spelling and hard work.

Other comments from longtime residents reveal similar sentiments.

One prairie resident of 101 years, Mera Andresen, simply states that nature works best; and our featured pioneer woman, Frances N. Jones, writes this: "Most of the things on the prairie are beautiful in their natural state. Leave the prairie in its natural state as much as possible." Oh how her sensible words ring true. But are we smart enough to listen, or will we refuse the prairie's offerings—peace, solace, happiness, personal growth, inspiration, and self-knowledge—in our haste to advance, to change.

As each new day dawns, remember, we are responsible for our own fate—the fate of our children, grandchildren. And in taking the prairie's discernible wisdom into our hearts, our souls, perhaps we should consider the words and ways of those who trod before us, because when the capacity to learn is lost, hope is lost. When a people, indeed, a land or a country, is without hope, joy will be fleeting, scarce, with no meaningful way to survive, to prosper.

Think about it.

There is no covered wagon for us to travel in, but there is new, unexplored territory just ahead. Let us remain open to learning, hopeful about our future, dedicated to the challenges of our time. Hopefully, the pioneer spirit will resonate within you as we continue to chart our course, as steep and arduous as each step may be, for there is no turning back.

Oh to dwell on the sweet past
Where most of my life is cast
A smile, a face, a time, a place,
There is so much to retrace.
Oh to walk that trail once more,
To redo the things I adore.
Misty eyed and with deep sigh,
I watch the reel of life go by.

~HAROLD H. SCHULER,
Pierre Since 1910

CHAPTER TWELVE
The Prairie Connection

V OLUMES HAVE BEEN WRITTEN about time: how to manage it, control it, use it, beat it, indeed, how to find more of it; nowadays it's nearly impossible to stop thinking about time. Clocks, calendars, and computers incessantly remind us of deadlines, priorities, appointments, and schedules; yet no matter what formula we adopt, what fad we embrace, very little changes when it comes to a perceived shortage of precious hours in each day.

The world, in most contexts, is a place of frenzy and frantic pursuit. *Hurry* has taken on new meaning, new urgency, and is often engrained in our minds at a young age, never to be forgotten, easily dismissed or countered. A friend explained that "hurry" rattles through his mind almost continually, in the background of his thoughts like a never ending freight train rumbling down a winding track with no final destination at all.

We hurry, we rush, we forget to say no. At times we run in circles, not knowing where the circle began, where, or if, it will end. You know the feeling, I'm sure. As mentioned in previous chapters, however, the prairie suggests a deeper, broader definition of time—one that moderates the exacting pressures of family, work, and society; one with a strong sense of renewal. While everyone around us seems to be asking something of us, the prairie seems to *give* us something. Organically, wholeheartedly.

This perspective has rubbed off on the people who live here; whenever possible we still take (and make) time for each other, so that basic values and honest needs of a very human variety remain in the forefront, not the next deadline, company meeting, country club function, or trip to the mall. While such things have their place, the prairie culture refuses to be controlled by anything other than the simple and compelling ways of the heart. In a place where continuity and quiet compassion predominate, the dividing line emerges naturally, almost magically, and from this sensitive stance, it's easier to keep egos in line—the environment, overall, is calmer, less rushed and impulsive and crazed with "go-here-now, be-there-now" mandates.

For one thing, the prairie culture, the people who comprise it, try to avoid unreasonable demands or expecting everyone to move at the same pace. In a place where nature calls the shots, people are less insistent about getting their way. Where caring for animals and crops often takes center stage, again, most people have come to accept delays, emergencies, and shifting priorities with a certain amount of aplomb. You get the feeling in talking to these people, those who grew up with the noticeable power of land and sky at their side, that it would take something major, even difficult to envision, to rattle them.

Too many roaring blizzards when livestock lost their lives, too many dry summers when crops struggled each day to survive, too many harsh days of strong wind when the dust blew free with a life of its very own. These factors have taken their toll, on these people, on this place, where the only sure thing is a strong, caring heart, so rushing around in a senseless battle to get everything done in precisely the right order simply lacks appeal. Most people have strong beliefs about what's important, what's not, so making the important things a priority comes more naturally.

Realistically, if their hearts aren't truly in something, it probably won't get done—not quickly, anyway. And not without a fair amount of grumbling.

Prairie Evenings

When was the last time you considered your personal priorities, besides when you read my chapter about fun? Does the outside world control your day, your night, your entire agenda: week to week, month to month, year to year? Are you stuck in a reactionary mode when you would rather be acting on your own needs, inclinations? Could the most important things be buried in an overwhelming mix of "what isn't important"?

Fortunately, I know of something called prairie vision.

The prairie view—the prairie contrast—mimics a peaceful nothingness that brings our lives back into focus. No matter what season, in this place where the heart resides there is some aspect of nature and the outdoors capable of pulling you away from your routine and worries while offering a broader, more personally fulfilling, perspective: one that puts you back in the driver's seat.

A few ideas: gaze deeply on a golden-tipped wheat field before harvest; let a fishing guide take you out on the Missouri when the water's sparkly surface emits streams of sunlit rays; soak up the sun on a warm autumn day when sunflowers droop in abundance; go sledding down a gently yielding prairie hill; find a pond with a thick cover of ice for skating; walk through the prairie on a bright spring day in search of your favorite wildflowers; pick some wild blackberries; take your sketch pad to a friend's ranch; explore unknown country roads. Anything that offers a reprieve from a hectic pace, the mundane, the millions of things you *must* do, the narrowing of vision that seems to occur as we repeat schedules and tasks and conversations ad infinitum. The prairie scene, in all its many incarnations, can fuel your imagination with pleasing, multidimensional images that speak directly to your soul.

The Prairie Connection

I'm again reminded of summer evenings, prairie evenings, when the outside world feels distant, almost nonexistent. Try to picture this in your mind's eye.

Almost leisurely, the sun is setting—the western sky, artistic stretches of amber and peach—and the air is warm, at least eighty degrees, with a slight June breeze, cattle and horses graze in a nearby pasture and a few meadowlarks chime in, their melodic call familiar, comforting. Surrounded by greenish-brown tall grass prairie (when pioneers traversed the Great Plains such grasses covered about one-third of America) swaying back and forth in rhythmical fashion, we walk toward the disappearing sun. Under our feet the ground is dry—we hear a crinkling noise as we walk, disturbing the coveted blanket of silence. Like mounds of fall leaves, the grasses silently welcome, offering beauty, natural strength, composure, certainty. Competing thoughts that cry out for attention like a long row of spoiled children have grown quiet; "do it faster, do it better, do it now" voices that seem to reverberate in your psyche also may have grown calm, taciturn. With the prairie's aura surrounding us, our thoughts have stopped swirling like overworked honeybees: Now you are the wise, knowing captain of your ship.

Essentially, you have come home to yourself, to a place you once knew but unknowingly abandoned in a maddening rush to get somewhere—to do what the swirl of faces and voices around you expected, told you was important. Taking time for ourselves (our inner world) is easily neglected, more so with the crushing demands of a hyper-competitive global society, so yes, it may take the sweet, innocent melody of a meadowlark to remind us of this need. How have we forgotten to spend time with ourselves; how have we ignored such an important need, postponed it or downgraded it? Maybe we have to hit the extremes before we get the message.

As a young person eager to explore the world beyond my surroundings, I mistakenly concluded that the prairie's pull was something to resist, as I couldn't understand why the immense lands, the windswept terrain without bright lights, apparent action or excitement, insisted on being such a strong force in my life. Why did the area have such a grip on my heart when it seemed time to be free of all that, to move on to other things—more visible, outward signs of life—that surely were more interesting?

As you may have guessed, the more I resisted the prairie's compelling spirit, the more I questioned its subtle teachings and truths, the more its essence echoed through my mind like the wise words of a grandparent, an insightful friend, refusing to be silenced.

But in my surrender, I discovered peace, happiness, contentment.

Unexpected, unexplained, yet true in every way.

With this liberating revelation, I realized something even more important: the time spent growing up in the middle of nowhere was an experience to be treasured, not overlooked or diminished by myself or anyone else who

The Prairie Connection

lacked appreciation for it. Like Thoreau's famous journey into the woods, the prairie—the life around it—is a good place to "live deliberately, to front only the essential facts of life."

I also realized that while the lands offering incredible beauty were not my enemy, neither were they as somber, silent, or passive as once perceived—seemingly uninvolved, unrelated to the world beyond. In some ways, this land was the world, everything else a mere artifact designed to support the nuances and demands of a modern day, a contemporary society. When I made that fruitful connection, yet another prairie truth fell into place.

It wasn't corny or unsophisticated to care deeply about an isolated land with few people and so little apparent "place" in a fast-paced, complex world. Even though visitors looking for man-made marvels that glitter and glow in the dark were easily turned off or intimidated or downright perplexed by the area (the wide-open spaces can make some feel jittery, mildly confused), I knew the understated power of place: understood its value to humankind.

As I came to terms with my prairie heart—its dictates, its wisdom, its trusted role in my life—it became increasingly clear to me that our lives should be filled with heart. If your heart has moved on, grown quiet or overly somber, it may be time to chart a more viable course. To settle for less implies several things: it will be difficult to identify the important things if your life has slipped into a dark, unhappy state; a life without heart is a disservice to society, holding others back, keeping people from seeing the deeper, more meaningful truths life is meant to reveal; and when there is a lack of heart, there is probably a lack of honesty (something isn't quite right, and usually we know it), and within this context, we cheat and belittle ourselves, blaming everything, everyone around us for an existence that is, at a minimum, not in harmony with the cosmos.

But then again, prairie life encourages an honest approach.

Unadorned, unencumbered, the land itself looks honest—its mighty heart visible to those who look closely. On a certain level, we are encouraged to assess what is important, what is not. As a symbol of life's natural simplicity—complete, pure, lofty yet down-to-earth—the land imparts a back-to-the-basics theme with the dignity and precision of a spiritual advisor, one who is trusted, one who knows the heart of every man, woman, and child regardless of race, religion, or family heritage. One who dares to speak the truth in the face of rejection, ridicule, or unkind hilarity.

This is the prairie's gift to us at the turn of the century and beyond. Not a useless, bleak land, as some may conclude prematurely, without deep understanding or exploration; rather, the boundless space, what it contains and symbolizes, is a gift without a price. Ideally, it would never be owned by those who don't see its timeless beauty; the prairie, in its natural state, is to be celebrated for all it represents—for what it has meant to so many generations. Even for the tears it has evoked from the hardiest of souls, and the sheer joy, the love, and the wonder the prairie inspires in us when we knowingly gaze upon it with understanding and appreciation.

I know of no more encouraging fact than the unquestionable ability of man to elevate his life by a conscious endeavour.

~HENRY DAVID THOREAU,
Walden

CHAPTER THIRTEEN
A Certain Brilliance

WHY DOES A RANCHER who can afford to go to the grocery store and buy as many chickens—frozen or fresh, chopped or whole—as he wants or needs, buy a crate of chicks? Yellow, fluffy, chirping, busily pecking around for seeds or bugs, oblivious to the charming little girl standing next to the wooden crate with a big smile on her face.

Why do people take pets—cats, dogs, birds—into their homes in record numbers; why do people around the globe devote countless hours as volunteers for worthwhile causes? What about the time we give to family members, to friends and hobbies, to neighbors and community events—no real mystery, is it?

Helping other people, things, or interests along is a global pastime; raising chicks is just one small example, a

Always Returning

prairie example. But consider how wonderful the experience is for a young child, boy or girl. Not because chickens are the most enchanting animals in the world necessarily, but because she will cherish the memories well beyond her childhood. He will learn firsthand the wonder of growth and development; she will experience the demands and responsibilities of caring for a helpless creature dependent on the outside world for survival. Prairie truths, that's all. Simple, basic facts that sometimes get lost in the everyday shuffle.

That, too, is a basic wonder of the prairie.

The good things, tested, tried, and true, that we know about life, the things that we know work, become more obvious and apparent in a setting that allows for greater visibility of the finer details—the connecting points in life that offer a rare glimpse into our shared humanity, our better selves. Patterns, often habits of unknown origin, when taken for granted or missed entirely in other settings stand out with a certain brilliance on the prairie. Even the small things like taking a step back to see the importance and value derived from helping a child raise some fluffy, yellow chicks in the spring.

An article in *South Dakota Magazine* called "Dakota Skies" shared a few thoughts from Robert Adams: stars in the distance, in the blackened prairie sky, can remind us of the good things in life. Things and people that, when nurtured, when cared for, have the power to reward us in intangible, surprising, ways. "All of us appreciate the Dakota skies which, clothed in sparkling stars by night and bathed in the light of a glorious sun by day, sustain our bond with nature and lift our view and thoughts to other things than the world's tears."

Do you set the stage, consciously or unconsciously, for this kind of surprise in your life, allowing for the magical, the miraculous; do you open your heart to the goodness of sharing yourself with others, more or less fortunate or on an equal plane? It makes no difference in the end; what counts is that you showed the heart, the good sense, to seize the moment: seeing and taking the opportunity to give of yourself in a meaningful way. The size and magnitude of the contribution isn't the issue; the process—the time, energy, and attention—that goes into something is what counts. Just being there for another person might be all it takes, or caring about someone who no one else is able to view in a positive (or deserving) light. Maybe it's a matter of giving someone a second or third chance.

One prairie resident said: "When you give of yourself it takes the focus off yourself . . . by doing this, the problems we face seem not so great." One man who lives close to the land mentions the satisfaction he gets from offering fatherly advice every now and then, how much he enjoys helping people better their lives; he talks about loaning money to a friend when he didn't really have the funds to spare. Our pioneer lady, Frances, believed "it is easier to give than to receive." Even when she was living through a tough time herself, when it might have been easier to have turned away, she felt she gained "peace of mind" from continuing to give of herself.

Always Returning

Once Frances rented a room to a man who was unable to pay the rent, but later on, he mailed her five dollars in every letter, eventually overpaying her.

"I was more than paid," she explains.

So when life seems dull and lackluster, or even when it seems particularly spectacular, there is something to be said, something powerful, for the healing, healthy ways of the heart. In a society, indeed a world, that serves up a strong dose of ill will each day, the prairie way reminds us of the need to "do good." As a carryover from the pioneer days, perhaps, or maybe because of the land itself—a strong yet subtle force in the lives of those who experience its sphere of influence—there remains a noticeable feeling of vulnerability on the prairie. Endearing, really.

Maybe even a bit charming, for the net effect creates a need among many residents to acknowledge the plight of every living person and creature to survive, to prosper, to make the best from the worst. And from this recognition springs a desire to help others, because in a place where cattle, horses, wind, immense wheat fields, prairie grass, and a heavenly sky predominate, no one dares to take on the elements alone.

Like courting disaster, an enormous ego doesn't last long on the prairie; someone or something is always prepared to trim it down to size. The prairie, its people, are realists at heart, contending with excess or false pride by reminding themselves and each other that hard times are just over the next hill. While it may not be true in the literal sense, life has a way of tossing out a mixed bag: no matter who you are, no matter where you live, no matter what you do. And while this isn't meant to imply that we should wallow in our own misery, welcoming misfortune as if it were a best friend, something we deserve, or worse yet, a reflection of an unlucky soul, a certain amount of peace and positive, life-enhancing energy is released when we accept the ways of the world by giving back to the Universe.

In a global society that often prides itself on *getting ahead*, and definitely at this point in our nation's history, it's also beneficial to consider the spiritual and emotional healing made possible by practicing this prairie dictum: Personal power, personal gain is best augmented by actively honoring the cyclical nature of the cosmos, because, seemingly, the world order seeks balance, harmony, and, curiously enough, stability within movement. So I, like many, can't help but sense the wisdom, indeed, the honor, that springs from acknowledging the unseen forces governing our existence. Consistently, wholeheartedly.

Intrinsic Value

When you unwrap a gift, what is at the heart of the package—something light and friendly, or an intimate, deeply felt gesture, or maybe something delightfully unique? With only rare exception, the true message, the point of the gift, reveals itself best on the inside; wrapping, a gift's exterior, is merely a cover, colorful paper suggesting a birthday, an anniversary, one of the many holidays or special occasions that arise. Even with an outrageous bow and curls of ribbon, it's the inside component that speaks to us. So it is when we give of ourselves. Our thoughts, intentions, concern and caring, perceptions, courage, and honesty—they all flow from the inside.

Words, for instance, when shared to convey ideas, feelings, beliefs, or encouragement possess amazing power; words can provide incredible gifts without measure or price. By providing a vehicle for what is on the inside, words, when written or spoken (sometimes unspoken, merely sensed), provide priceless commodities: freedom, dignity, choice, love, passion, or the rich empathy of friendship. Often, they communicate compassion or insights. Maybe a secret worry, a doubt that feels overwhelming when held inside, isolated from the world, or fears, sorrow and sadness, frustration or confusion. *Anything and everything.*

Yet how often do we overlook the power of words to shape and define our lives, to guide our children, to lessen our fears?

Instead, when giving to others, we too often turn to the external world; we give others the wrapping without the contents. Send cards from gift shops with nothing more than a signature, without a handwritten note that comes from the heart; we buy something we like that has no meaning for the recipient; we throw a party out of a sense of duty or obligation, to impress the neighbors perhaps, when heartfelt words that convey understanding, concern, and appreciation might have meant more.

While there is a time, a place, for such things, in our curious haste to keep up, follow the crowd, fit in or adhere to the latest fad, we succumb to external pressures and visions that, when used indiscriminately, don't help us build bridges; rather, they weaken or even destroy them. As a people, as an ever-expanding world, we don't seem to have accepted the limited role of artificial constructs, external aids, that are incapable of providing warmth, respect, meaningful connection, and love. When, for instance, was the last time you paid someone a compliment—one you meant, one that required perception and awareness of the individual on an internal level, one he or she remembered or even shared with someone else?

I'm reminded of a popular movie, As *Good as It Gets*, and the scene where Carol (Helen Hunt) asks Melvin (Jack Nicholson) to pay her a compliment—right now, or she's gone. As is fitting to the role, he hems and haws, looks skyward, rolls his eyes, and so on as he tries to come up with an acceptable response. Finally, and surprisingly, Melvin explains that she makes him try to be a better man. And later in the movie, near the end, when he's still trying to convince her that he's for real, not just an eccentric author looking for a vulnerable catch to boost his shaky ego, he shares his deepest impressions of her, telling Carol he is able to see below the surface to what is so special and wonderful about her . . . on the inside.

Of course, she melts.

And the movie winds down to its expected happy ending at the neighborhood bakery at four in the morning, before dawn has immersed the city streets in activity—in the external world. A powerful example of the incredible agility of words, of being able to perceive a deeper truth, the innate goodness and humanity within another person, indeed, this is as "good as it gets." And in terms of forging a heartfelt bond of long-term duration between two people, very little seems to compare with the couple's ability to see and appreciate the essence, what is on the inside, at the center, the core, of each other—the part most people overlook, fail to understand, or largely misconstrue.

Prairie life sets a good example for this, though. By persistently encouraging us to look beneath the obvious for what is real, we're reminded to give others something of intrinsic value; we are reminded to give of ourselves.

A Childhood Diary

As a young person, I, like most people, recorded my private thoughts in a diary or journal, usually promptly discarded as fear *(who might find this?)* won out against *it might be fun to look back and read this someday.* And one day, when my mother mentioned she'd happened across her old Girl Scout diary, one from her elementary school years, I thought about this again. Amazed to find it, she enjoyed the memories her discovery provided.

It occurs to me now that if others noticed the things about us we wish they would see or come to understand, childhood diaries might not be such a secret, such a worry, such a risk. But we've created a society of strangers in many respects, and only history can inform us of the net effect. If we shared more from our internal worlds, however, maybe we'd find there is little to fear but fear itself, as someone famous said. And maybe we'd find our way back to our hearts, our only lasting salvation perhaps.

Obviously, I'm not advocating the careless, indiscriminate, or insensitive dissemination of personal feelings or thoughts—rather, sharing just enough to keep us real in the eyes of others. We live in a world of some danger, hidden or manifest, so our safety, the well-being of others, is of critical importance. Yet if we succumb to our fears without a fight, or go overboard in creating layers and layers of protection, perhaps we are merely supporting the forces that would destroy our very humanity—something glorious and fine and most worthy of our protection.

Another movie, *Patch Adams,* comes to mind. Starring Robin Williams and based on a true story, he plays a medical student committed to change. Patch makes it his personal crusade to improve the quality of life for patients and puts up a valiant effort to alter the "system." In the movie, he confronts a lot of fear, and, of course, meets with considerable resistance; but he does prevail, to a point. Doing so, he's an inspiration, revealing what we are all capable of in our finer moments.

Basically, he is fighting for people—medical patients—to be treated with basic regard and dignity so their emotional and spiritual needs will also be accounted for in an environment dedicated to their healing. His approach makes tremendous sense, and is symptomatic of broader issues in contemporary cultures. As we move farther and farther away from the "human element," due to the serious issues that plague our civilization at the dawn of the twenty-first century, we further jeopardize our future with each waking breath.

It's indeed an appropriate time to glance back at the pioneers of the prairie, at the men and women who shaped this country, to ask ourselves, *where in the world are we going*? Are we losing our capacity to care, or is there simply too much to care about? What can we do to change things before it is too late? Look inside your heart for the answers; share your truth. As Thoreau reminds us: "Say what you have to say, not what you ought. Any truth is better than make-believe."

*I learned a prairie secret:
take the numbing distance in small doses
and gorge on the little details that beckon.*

~WILLIAM LEAST HEAT-MOON,
PrairyErth

CHAPTER FOURTEEN
Zoom Lens

T HIS BOOK WOULDN'T BE COMPLETE without consideration of the seemingly insignificant details in life—inconspicuous, layered, laced throughout—that are easily overlooked in the whirlwind pace, the fast lane, the spellbinding dance that engrosses and absorbs us, mesmerizing our tired minds until we lack the ability, the will, to *see* the details.

Of course, on a basically flat land with nothing but rolling prairie for backdrop, where people and trees are treasured commodities, little things aren't so very little. A matter of context, but also quite revealing because of the enhanced focus, the balanced perspective, which is consistently nurtured. These aren't people who have already seen it all—not according to mainstream definitions of what is *in*, what is *out*.

Always Returning

What they have seen, however, is *this:* the inspiring survival of livestock, gardens, crops, and fledgling trees when things looked hopeless; relentless snows, punishing winds, and parched earth, dry and rock hard but somehow renewable each spring; pinkish morning skies that tease the imagination, stretching overhead with the promise of something other than intense, blistering heat. People of the prairie, those who take active note of their surroundings, in particular, have witnessed life at its most fundamental, sometimes less than glorious, sometimes marvelous and miraculous level.

And from this rather lofty perch, many have relinquished the need to submit to society's standards, of what it supposedly means to live. Instead, many have yielded to the powers that be, and in taking the prairie into their hearts and lives, their vision is restored; they are empowered to see the world from a position of strength, quiet, and calm. Not a mad dash to follow the crowd, a circus act intended to elicit cheers, laughter, and applause, the prairie culture is more apt to reward and nurture an attitude of appreciation for the priceless, often innocent, details inherent in the milieu all mortals share.

Life-sustaining details seen with clarity and precision, when viewed intently, closely, as if through a zoom lens, can somehow renew a belief in the value and natural beauty of life: a new calf or colt, apple trees blanketed in white in the spring, a robin eager to display its squirming catch after a morning shower, a field of vibrant sunflowers, faces turned toward a golden sun. Maybe a tiny bow in

Zoom Lens

a child's hair, the hesitant notes of a first piano recital, or the unexpected smile of an elderly man in a wheelchair. Sometimes it's nothing more than the quiet lisp of moving water, a light breeze running through cottonwoods, camouflaged deer or pheasant, bare branches thick with morning frost, a lilac bush bursting with color.

A prairie list is endless and would include all of the above and more.

Yet how often do we forget, or fail, to look, to *see* the mighty details of life so capable of enlarging our sense of self and well-being?

It's not unusual to rush by and over them to accomplish the so-called important things; yet I have to wonder if we aren't missing the picture entirely. When life gets out of focus there is a common tendency to turn, or run, away, to slight, even disconnect from priorities, people, and established purposes that are at the core of existence until something happens to bring us back to our senses. Until something points us back to the proper view.

Ideally, from my perspective the proper view is one where the incidental side of things, the part discounted by those who have lost sight of the value of life's most sacred, awe-inspiring moments, isn't brushed away or hastily tucked in around the edges. Where common moments that embody the spirit of existence generate a smile, a pat on the back, a wink reflecting shared understanding, appreciation.

The prairie view is of the soul-wise variety—not from purposeful design necessarily and not because of modern-era books instructing prairie dwellers on how to put more soul into their lives. Rather, the soul-wise ways of many of these people naturally reflects a humble, unpretentious attitude that has been around a long time. Sustained and finely honed by the elements, by the economies of a rural environment in the middle of nowhere, by a vast terrain that is loved by many as though a member of their family, the prairie's soul has had its rightful say:

> *In gazing out upon me look not for Bright Lights; look not for the magnificence of the Golden Gate Bridge, the power of the Statue of Liberty, imposing mountaintops or masterful ocean tides; but gaze out upon me for comfort and inspiration against the harshness of the world. And in so doing know that the lessons of this land are many, its triumphs seemingly few, its sorrows often unbearable. Yet the wildflowers of the prairie still bloom each spring as gentle breezes still whistle through the prairie grass with a melodic, peaceful sound, as all sorts of wildlife rustle around looking for a safe haven, as time marches on into the next century. As the morning dawns and the soul is once again awakened to another day, another love, another time.*

With Mother, bread baking was an art, and mother would bake 8–12 loaves twice a week. She used her own live yeast, a sponge of yeast, potato water, shortening, salt, flour . . . mixing and letting it rise at night.

~LORNA BUNTROCK HERSETH,
Autobiography

CHAPTER FIFTEEN
Spice It Up

FROM THE STANDBYS that most of us depend on to elaborate affairs featuring the finest menus, food preparation and consumption play central roles in our lives: physical survival, a sense of purpose and a predictable routine, companionship with family and friends, a traditional backdrop for social events, and, for some, a creative outlet. Not surprisingly, this sometimes mundane aspect of life also gives us an avenue for emotional expression and caring, for linking hearts and minds as we define our lives.

Imagine the countless number of relationships forged over food: extravagant, mildly interesting to plain boring. It doesn't seem to matter. As a primary building block dating back to the inception of life, nurturing ourselves and those around us with food we enjoy comes naturally. Like emotional, spiritual, and intellectual sustenance, there is a positive connection between sharing culinary talents and a renewal of our physical energies. On the prairie, in the city, no matter where you reside, this is a simple fact of life, one we recognize and accept without further thought. At this point in history, it's worthwhile and interesting, however, to consider the troubling changes taking place in our midst: multitudes of fast-food chains, demanding schedules that prompt us to "drive through," prepackaged grocery items with a list of ingredients unknown to man or woman, rushed dinner hours turned into minutes, fewer *shared* meals with meaningful conversation and genuine human interaction.

Granted, some of these societal adjustments can be linked to bigger, broader changes taking place all around us, and we have to keep up . . . to a point. Yet if we hope to be masters of our own destiny, at least to a useful degree, then why not look at this from a soul-wise perspective? Why not query our hearts for guidance?

There is merit in asking ourselves if we are comfortable with a drive-through world, with lessened emphasis on preparing food from natural ingredients in a manner that is satisfying and pleasing to the heart and soul, with an "always in a hurry" atmosphere around the table, in front of the television, in the car, or standing in the kitchen. Excess time is a luxury most of us don't have, so "quick and easy" appeals to many, yet in moments of silent worry or frustration, do you ever feel like you inadvertently signed up for the wrong race, one you didn't intend to participate in?

Spice It Up

Do you practically inhale your lunch, skip it entirely, or eat something you don't enjoy in the slightest—to hurry through the process, to get lunch behind you and quickly move on to the next task, or obligation? It happens; you aren't alone.

But let's peer into the prairie scene once again; perhaps there is a bit of wisdom lurking there if we look carefully at a lifestyle still "catching up" with the rest of the world. And in glancing back, in studying a culture based on its own set of tried and true values, maybe we will come across a few ideas guaranteed to have a place in your life, too. Because the time to look is *now*, before unwanted, unhealthy patterns become ingrained in your lifestyle.

A Prairie Cook

What is a prairie cook? What does he look like, what role does cooking play in his daily life? Stepping back to the days of threshing crews, large families of ten or so children, and groups of cowboys riding together as they worked this or that ranch, a prairie cook was just about anyone who would take the job!

Short or tall, young or old, man or woman, married or single—if you could fry an egg, make a cup of coffee, your future was secure. And if you could start a fire in the middle of nowhere—without causing a prairie fire—so much the better. Supplies were rudimentary, consisting of must-have items only. Blackened pots and pans, a handful of dented tin cups, a cast-iron skillet, maybe a couple of bowls and a metal ladle for soup.

Always Returning

Time marched on, of course, and before long the prairies were dotted with more people, more hardy souls, and since men were usually needed outside, cooking became a female specialty. Some took to the task as if the sun wouldn't shine without their hard work and fierce dedication, but others caved under the pressure, leaving the heavy cooking to those next in line: aunts, sisters, daughters, mothers, grandmothers. But brothers and uncles, some willing cousins, and quite likely a stranger, "just passing through," could win a spot in the kitchen, too, as the workload, for many prairie cooks, was grueling.

Eventually conditions improved, but the demand for good cooks, for food preparation in substantial quantities, prevailed. Cooking for sizeable groups was a highly valued skill well into recent times. In certain settings, it's still an ability worth acquiring. In spring, summer, and fall, large farming and ranching operations hire extra help, "hired hands," for harvesting or branding livestock, but nowadays, the ranch owner's wife usually gets the responsibility for feeding the "help," for providing large quantities of food morning, noon, and night.

Of course, she is free to recruit additional help—if she can!

All in all, a prairie cook was any brave soul who had a talent for keeping food warm, a good sense of humor (most would rather laugh than cry), a willingness to serve a group of less than gracious or sophisticated people, often men with voracious appetites, hungry and impatient, and

Spice It Up

a rare ability to work and cook with whatever was available—to improvise without complaint. I almost forgot—this individual was willing to work for so-so wages or room and board. Or, in the case of a lucky spouse who had become the resident prairie cook, for nothing more than a hurried smile, a quick "thanks" offered on the way out the door.

You're right, of course: The job, the role, was not particularly glamorous.

Yet from this not so enviable vantage point, prairie cooks have passed down, through the generations, impressions and qualities worth considering, even now—into this new century. And those who may not qualify as prairie cooks, women and men who only cook for small families, or just for themselves, with modern conveniences also have something to offer. For recipes circulate like dollar bills on the prairie, where there is still plenty of emphasis on homemade cooking and all the heartwarming things that go with it: colorful gardens, a mix of vegetables and flowers; canned, baked, and pickled goods; potlucks featuring a variety of hot dishes; family recipes and cooking traditions passed down for generations.

Wileta Hawkins, mother to three sons and a "pioneer" in her own right, put together two family cookbooks. She told me that one of her favorite recipes was her mother's cream pie. Here it is: *Mix together 2 cups heavy cream, 1 cup sugar, ½ cup flour, and 2 teaspoons vanilla, then pour into an unbaked pie shell and bake 30 minutes at 350 degrees just until golden brown.*

Prairie Art

Good cooking is a cherished form of prairie art; the opportunity to share talent, resources, affection, and companionship adds to its creative appeal and makes it central to the lifestyle. If a neighbor is down on his or her luck, if there is cause to celebrate, if someone's garden has produced massive quantities of rhubarb, cucumbers, tomatoes, or corn, most will gladly see this as a chance to step into the kitchen. Not out of a sense of duty or obligation, but from a desire to nurture others in a way that comes naturally.

There is something unpretentious about it.

It fits the place like a charm, a perfect prairie charm, one that sustains a belief in the value of what is attainable and realistically satisfying. *Everyday value* that enhances daily life in a way that is reminiscent of bygone days when life on the prairie was a survival test in every sense of the word. (There are those who would argue that life on the prairie is *still* a test to survive, and depending on occupation, goals, or personal preferences, that may be the case.) But in backyards, on farms of all sizes, there are also bountiful gardens that produce the most gorgeous fruits and vegetables. And flowers grown as garden borders add a special brilliance to the welcoming scene. As if planted with tremendous care by those drawn to a pleasing mix of summer colors—white, purple, orange, blue, yellow—garden flowers add a special touch.

Nothing out of the ordinary typically; if you were to tour a few prairie gardens, you would probably find fragrant marigolds, beds of petunias, hollyhocks standing tall, purple and white iris, sunny chrysanthemums, and maybe tiger lilies. A few rosebushes may grace the land, as well, but they will be a hardy variety designed to survive a prairie winter.

Tucked in many yards are wild rosebushes thick with pink and yellow blooms, lilac bushes, and spirea with dainty white flower clusters on slender stems. Wild rosebushes are my favorite, but please don't compare wild roses to the long-stemmed variety that require careful attention, for wild roses have a natural, spontaneous beauty that can't be duplicated.

Covered with thorns, however, pruning the wild rosebush can be a small challenge; and keep in mind as you clip some delicate blooms for a bowl of roses that bees love these too. Their fragrance is fresh, clear, perfume-like, and full of allure. But wild roses can be difficult, if not impossible, to transplant. With a long taproot, you'll need to offer this rosebush plenty of quiet appreciation if you want it to adapt to a new location with any degree of success. I hope it's easy to see how the area comes to life through the beauty people create in informal gardens, how the prairie, *as a place*, endears itself to us.

Good food, often traditional, cooks who delight in working with their hands, hearts, and souls to produce pleasing dishes for long-awaited guests, spur-of-the-moment company, and family members, along with a spirit of adventure, are hallmarks of the prairie kitchen. One woman I interviewed told me that birthday cakes were her specialty, while others made note of the companionship and closeness that cooking provided. My mother, who we teased by calling her "Betty Crocker," could have—in younger years—danced circles around any big city chef.

Some of her specialties were blueberry pancakes with a hint of cinnamon, caramel rolls that her grandchildren said were good enough to "die for," rhubarb-strawberry pie with a touch of lemon, and tonight, rummaging through recipes passed down over the years, I see one for Aunt Sally's Beer Pancakes. But I don't dare discuss her chocolate cake, which wasn't for the weak of heart, but her only secret, so she said, was to follow the directions (if you're a beginner) and put your heart into the task at hand so others will sense the attention—the time, thought, and special skill—that went into it.

Now, as I picture her in the family kitchen at all times of the day and busily focused on whatever she was preparing, apron pulled tight, hair pushed back from her face, which was sometimes red when she was really moving, I recall the countless hours devoted to cooking, and hope we didn't take it for granted. Although, I suppose, like most children, we did.

She enjoyed it—time always flies when I'm cooking, she'd say—and it seemed so natural and easy for her that I'm quite confident we failed to remember that this was still work. Her skill and assuredness in the kitchen, the obvious pleasure cooking and baking gave her, made it easy for us to forget.

Spice It Up

Lemon Meringue Pie

I grew up with three younger sisters, one brother, and since all of us learned how to cook—a necessity in my mother's eyes—as adults, we are at home in the kitchen. But none of us ever mastered lemon meringue pie, another one of my mother's specialties.

A beautiful sight when prepared correctly, it has a certain zesty appeal, I guess. But it's such a touchy pie, such a tricky recipe, that many people, including myself, are intimidated by it.

Here is my mother's favorite recipe: *Microwave for 4 to 5 minutes 1.5 cups sugar, ⅓ cup cornstarch, 1.5 cups water. In small bowl beat 3 egg yolks, add some of the hot mixture to the eggs, stir, then add remaining yolks to hot mixture and cook 2 more minutes. Add ¼ cup lemon juice, 1 tablespoon butter, pour in baked crust. For the meringue you need the 3 egg whites, ¼ teaspoon cream of tartar, 5 to 6 tablespoons sugar, a dash of vanilla. Beat the whites and tartar until frothy, adding sugar slowly, until mixture is firm, shiny. Add vanilla, gently put meringue on top of the pie filling. Brown in 350-degree oven for 15 minutes.*

That's it! So simple, I'm told.

I'll never share this with my mother, but I'm pretty sure I don't like lemon meringue pie. Could that be part of my reluctance, my fear of tackling this yellow-and-white dessert, which is hardly a prairie basic? That I'll have to ponder.

*No one is dissatisfied, not one is demented
with the mania of owning things....*

~WALT WHITMAN,
"SONG OF MYSELF"

CHAPTER SIXTEEN
Borrow It, Don't Buy It

SELF-SUFFICIENCY HAS ITS PLACE, yet like any plus, this mode of operation can become a minus when taken to extremes. Absolute independence from those in our midst, even if possible, would insulate and contain us well beyond healthy dimensions. Needing other people, other proclivities and opinions, and sources of emotional and intellectual support, as long as not excessive, forces us to reach out: keeps us humble, connected to forces outside, and beyond, ourselves.

Most of us realize that relationships of all shapes, sizes, origins, and destinations provide emotional fuel for our earthly journey: by giving us an opportunity to return the gift of caring and concern; by nurturing us through the storms of life; by helping us pilot our way across nebulous skies. Without human interaction, the gentle, abiding flow of wants, wishes, and worries comprising the silky web of life—its precarious stretch, its invisible dangle and sway from limb to limb—there would be a predictable collapse of all we hold dear; our days on earth floating away in meaningless bits and pieces like amorphous pieces of cotton drifting free from cottonwood trees in August. And what a sad state of affairs it would be, for built into our psyches is the very natural, very human need to experience ourselves in relation to others, to discover our own unique truths through the people we encounter during a lifetime.

We test our strengths, uncover our weaknesses, dismiss or overcome our limitations, celebrate our accomplishments, recover from our misconceptions, all within the context of *we*. So why do we stumble around in the dark trying to go it alone when a joint effort, the group or team approach, could smooth and show the way?

And, as is the stated focus of this chapter, why do we insist on buying everything instead of sharing resources more readily with others? Is it possible we've forgotten the lessons of old, prairie lessons about the value of lending a helping hand, of loaning or giving something away without strings, expectations, or strong feelings of ownership?

Overall, are we too attached to what we own, the ideas we have, the skills we possess, the wisdom we've gleaned and assimilated along the way, maybe even our love and concern for those around us, for humanity? Do we hold on to these things—these aspects of ourselves—waiting for the right occasion, the right moment, to share them; do we also fail to share our feelings and thoughts on the most cursory of levels?

Borrow It, Don't Buy It

While this may read like twenty questions, there is only one question at the heart of the matter: As a civilization, are we overly competitive, to the point of being destructive?

Everyone seems to crave and thrive on competition these days—beating out the next guy, getting there first, showing someone up—yet this fierce path seems to be taking us farther away from our finer, nobler, human qualities, and to me, these are admirable attributes worth preserving. Like the prairie lands, however, if we fail to place a value on life-enhancing, life-preserving ways of being, disintegration and eventual extinction may follow.

When our nation was young, when the settlers moved west filled with hopes and dreams (and yes, fears), they seemed to cling to a strong belief in themselves, but many knew the value of interdependence, of being able to rely on others for material or emotional support when the need arose. Survival, of paramount concern, encouraged and required faith in others, but the prairie mind-set, in a general sense, seemed to be one of realistic regard for life's unpredictable turns, and thus the eventual need to reach out for assistance. In short, borrowing necessary items or products was okay, simply confirming the ways of the world, the natural law of averages.

In sensing the shared nature of their precarious journey, neighbors helped each other and valued the need to be needed, of being able to reciprocate when the time came. Sometimes I think they gathered strength from this recognition, from their own form of self-sufficiency. By banding together, by helping people out in a spirit of survival, there was less emphasis on competition, less dependency on store-bought items (assuming they could find a store in the first place), but since that era, as we all know, things have changed.

Now we rush to the store almost automatically, wanting to pick out what is new, novel, or expensive: to impress someone, to stay on top of the latest fashions (trendy items do sell), to merely have something to do, and of course, to buy what we perceive as necessary. The act of purchasing, however, seems to have taken on a life of its own, and by giving some a false sense of independence, the cycle is self-perpetuating.

It has been my continuing observation, though, that a better balance could be achieved between borrowing and buying. This isn't to recommend making a nuisance of yourself, but to keep energy flowing, to keep relationships vital, there is merit in reducing the number of "things" you absolutely must own. And in lightening your load, the items you dust and carry around from room to room, the things you trip over, box up, or only keep out of a sense of obligation, a simpler lifestyle may present itself as an unexpected reward, an added benefit.

You may even feel more relaxed and comfortable, as if finally sailing away from a dark place you never liked much in the first place, free at last.

The Right Tone

If we can control our need to buy everything, to own everything, we can become pioneerlike, and maybe, at

Borrow It, Don't Buy It

this stage of our planetary and human evolution, that is a significant blessing—a highly desirable outcome. By returning to forgotten times and ways, gingerly picking up the threads that made sense (and still do), a powerful ray of hope can be generated. One that focuses the picture anew; that signals us in new directions, cleverly reminding us once again that less is more.

One prairie resident, when asked about this concept, said: "People are always borrowing, a pair of jumper cables for a dead battery, a pair of shoes. It's just something you do. You lend things when someone needs something, borrow if you need to."

A similar comment came from rancher and businessman Myril John Arch (deceased June of 2013). "When I first started on this ranch in 1954, I had only one horse and had to borrow the neighbor's horse to round up cattle. Not really resourceful," he adds, "just didn't have the money to buy another one."

Either way, borrowing, because it seems convenient, friendly, and fun, or borrowing out of necessity, can keep our need for material possessions in perspective. Regardless of where you reside, of where you have come to know the wisdom of place, develop close friendships that allow for a healthy give-and-take. The mutual respect, the warm feelings of cooperation that develop, will ensure a happier tomorrow for us all.

*I guess the interesting things that happen make life worth living.
Some are unhappy, but we can't pick and choose.*
~FRANCES NICKEL JONES,
South Dakota resident, 1895–2002

CHAPTER SEVENTEEN
The Merits of Challenge

Have you ever known someone who strikes you as living in a superficial realm? She (or he) seems out of touch with the complexities of life, continually seeking ways to ease her way through the day instead of grappling with meaningful challenges; he skims along the surface of life, too, never daring to commit to difficult, yet inspiring, goals; appears content to while away a lifetime seeking pleasure and entertainment to the exclusion of seizing opportunities for personal growth and development—situations, experiences beyond comfort zones.

And strangely enough, even when life deals such individuals a hand of dicey cards, they laugh it off, stubbornly refusing to accept any turn of events that doesn't match their world view, their happy-go-lucky existence. Usually, however, a catalyst appears on the horizon, one that mandates a significant amount of change, and to a degree at least, those who shun the more demanding side of life are eventually presented with a set of circumstances, often difficult and trying, that must be addressed. And only after trying to wiggle away do they succumb to the inevitable, digging deep within to uncharted territory—to priceless inner resources previously dormant, untapped.

These events are wake-up calls, and when impacted by them, we're often surprised by what we discover: courage, self-discipline, determination, new skills, compassion, personal insight, and self-awareness. In fact, experiencing an emotional or physical jolt that can't be ignored (confronting ourselves under dark, challenging conditions), we may encounter the true texture of life: the depth and richness and purpose of our lived experience. Trying times are often door openers—to ourselves and those around us, to a life that is compelling in its own right—and even though we may not want to pass through a particular door, one that has, in some respects, been identified and opened for us (too painful, too foreign and frightening, too dark and dismal), a sort of assurance and comfort can be derived by venturing onward, through the dreaded passageway.

Often the anticipation is worse than the reality.

When rough waters are navigated, intangible benefits, such as confidence, self-respect, and greater personal strength can be garnered from the journey, and when employed (and enjoyed) in the many contexts that emerge thereafter, such attributes carry enormous, life-altering

The Merits of Challenge

potential. Such character-building experiences are indeed worthy of our pursuit.

The moral of the story is simple. It's one we know *instinctively*, yet it's also one we tend to shy away from.

We are the sum of our experiences, and in seeking meaningful challenge, like the pioneers of the late 1800s, we are given an opportunity to expand, to discover who and what we are, to test our limits and beliefs, to succeed when the odds are against us, to try valiantly when failure, perceived or actual, is our only reward, to come to know the shape of our integrity, all so we have a chance to eventually understand what we're made of, on the inside. When our only significant goal is the desire to exist in a state of continual comfort, if it were even possible, the world fluctuates around us like a mystical, maniacal maze: our internal compass forever frozen at *safe*.

Mistakes Work

A challenge can be too difficult, too steep; we all have our limits and limitations, our hang-ups and our frailties, actual or perceived disabilities to consider and work around. For these we lament: *Oh, woe is me*. And sometimes we disavow these parts of ourselves. Occasionally, we pinpoint specific dimensions of our being for an overhaul, a New Year's resolution type of approach: *From here on out, I will watch less television, consume less sugar, write more love letters, work more puzzles, fly more kites, exercise daily, expand my mind, read more books, walk the dog each morning, call Uncle Floyd at least once a year. I'll even quit polluting the*

Always Returning

earth unnecessarily. And starting soon, I'll begin the project that has been on my mind, my mental to-do list, for months, the one that will be difficult to finish. I'll do more volunteer work, too, appreciate what the world has given me, share it with others who are less fortunate.

With echolike dependability, these words, *our* words, zing through our minds looking for a place to land. Yet for some reason they never find a permanent place to stop, only a temporary, sometimes momentary, place to pause until we are sidetracked, distracted by all that goes on around us, within us, or in spite of us. Still, the process, even though we may question the end result, offers us something real: a chance to fail, to forget, to question and rethink an answer, *to make a mistake.*

If there is one thing most societies seem to have a low tolerance for, this is it. Not to be used at random or to excess as an excuse for everything under the sun, making a mistake is completely normal. Yet even honest mistakes seem to make many people genuinely nervous and annoyed. Wonderful tools to help us learn more about our inner worlds, a few mistakes now and then are nothing but beneficial. Obviously, I'm not focusing on the sort of mistake that results in tragedy or any extreme, but without a misstep here and there, an unintentional slip, we will never know if the challenge is too difficult; we will not know how to modify our course of action or how to accomplish anything of real significance.

Like lights on an airport runway, mistakes help us identify the true path so we can aim ourselves in the right

The Merits of Challenge

direction. As life's indicators, our acceptance of the need to make mistakes can propel us forward. Growth, in fact, depends on an ability and a willingness to reach out, to err, and to modify behaviors, styles, or beliefs, and then to reach out again, letting the cycle redefine us until, eventually, over time, we replace the raw material with elements of wisdom.

Consider the multitude of mistakes the pioneers must have made; think about their hard-earned badges of courage; try to visualize their struggle to survive, the fears and problems that threatened to snuff out their dreams. Character-defining moments—plenty of them—were built into their existence, and while they suffered at times because of their mistakes, there is every reason to believe in the magic, in the poetry, of the accomplishment or self-understanding that manifested as a result of something quite fundamental: trial and error.

We are never totally above it, never totally beyond it, not until we are out of the game, our last breath taken. So why not zero in on a challenging goal, make it yours, give it your all? Find out if it's really too difficult or just deceptively so—there *is* a difference.

Grace Notes

Modern-day prairie dwellers, while not at the mercy of the outdoors, the untamed wilderness, to the same extent as those who traveled before them nonetheless live in a place that seeks them out. That is the distinct impression one gets in traversing the land. There is something about the openness that exposes and illuminates, causing some newcomers to feel vaguely uncomfortable. Slightly vulnerable. Curiously present. And within this level of visibility, within the prairie's radar screen, hiding places are few; it can feel as if there is nothing to shield you from the prying eyes of the Universe.

So life, in all its many shades, must be dealt with.

Even death, all the forces of nature that are awesome in their magnitude, splendid in their magnificence, ask to be recognized, no exceptions granted.

This feeling, this phenomenon, suggests a silent challenge: *Can you survive . . . here? Can you learn to love this vast terrain with its unpredictable ways? Can you accept the isolation, the contact and confrontation with prairie rattlers, wildlife that seems to own the place? Can you convince others of my worth, protect this land from those who would destroy it? And can you grow in compassion, grace, and dignity?*

When we really listen, it's amazing what we can hear.

I am large, I contain multitudes.

~WALT WHITMAN,
Leaves of Grass

CHAPTER EIGHTEEN
Generous Spirit

P RAIRIE MANNERS ARE NEATLY tucked into a generous, warmhearted way of life, and the focus is on genuine interaction that endears no matter what the occasion. Not in an artificial, short-lived way, not in a phony, textbook fashion, and clearly not in an effort to win the etiquette award for the year, but in a comfortable, friendly way.

Prairie manners aren't fancy or contrived.

While you may find a few minor distinctions based on class—true of most cultures in the world—there remains an underlying sameness to interactions that manifest as manners. The thread that joins the external realm with the internal state is the generosity of spirit that runs through the heart of those who reside on the prairie lands I grew up with. People who love to share whatever good fortune comes their way don't stop giving when times aren't wonderful, when misfortune arrives. It's not their nature, for the most part, nor would it be true to their character. These terms may sound synonymous, but there is a subtle difference.

Perhaps a matter of degree only, a question of to-what-extent-exactly, but it occurs to me that while we are likely born with our character, we can still make adjustments to our nature. And this makes room for something critical to our existence, namely, hope. I mention this again here because one thing we need, as a people, a culture, a society, and a civilization, is hope. It's the spark of the world's future, the reason we get up each day, and the absolute point of meaningful, worthwhile goals. Some degree of hope is at the root of nearly everything we do—if you stop and think about it.

Without hope, how can we *hope* to change, and without change, we're likely to repeat our questionable, less-than-admirable actions forever. In other words, there would be little point in discussing the generous spirit of prairie dwellers if this fine quality could not be emulated. And so it is that the invaluable worth of a generous spirit comes to light.

Walt Whitman put it well when he said: "When I give, I give myself."

In choosing to support others—giving of ourselves when it would be easier to turn away, taking time to care about the world and the people who inhabit it—we acknowledge the need for hopeful ways. Commensurate with the presence of nature, its mysterious force, without *hope* the day, quite possibly, could not be endured. Pioneers and

Generous Spirit

prairie dwellers learned to give themselves and each other the gift of hope.

Within this framework, they watched themselves grow, saw their dreams take root. With equal enthusiasm, they saw those they supported along the way break new ground, as well: succeed and survive when the gods threw every curve ball imaginable. So today, as an overall observation, this orientation continues, and while some see this trait as compensatory, something those who live on the prairie—in the middle of nowhere—engage in because they are unsophisticated hayseeds, because they lack the finer graces, or because they are naive or unworldly, nothing could be more inaccurate.

In giving to others, even when conventional wisdom dictates otherwise, prairie lore, in being true to itself, suggests an enlightened approach—one that springs from the heart and soul of its own accord. One longtime resident shared her thoughts on the subject, indicating that time and time again, whenever she reaches out to someone, she is rewarded.

In particular, she recounts a situation when she invited someone into her circle of friends, only to discover this person was going through a difficult time and thereby benefited greatly from her offer of support, friendship. How easy it is to envision a different scenario had she been afraid to extend an invitation, had she been worried about appearing foolish, assuming, or needy. "It just goes to show" (a familiar phrase in Dakota) that the wisdom of the world, the popularized, untested variety, is often a source of unwisdom.

Always Returning

It's fortunate that most people who live here hang on to their beliefs, even when the inevitable influences filter in, causing some to question their ways, values, and style—momentarily. Even when they know some are making fun of them because they seem old-fashioned, silly, corny, or any of the other clichés that circulate, many simply look the other way, a choice most are happy to make. Living up to personal standards and expectations is more important than appearing sophisticated, refined.

Not about to trade in their way of life for popular approval, brownie points, or anything smacking of a sellout, it would take a leveraged buyout to get a majority of these people to adopt a set of values that lacked a generosity of spirit. All year round, too, not just during holiday seasons.

But that can be fun to consider, too.

As these lines from a poem by Karen H. Wee in *The Book of Hearts* suggest, Christmas celebrations on the prairie often resulted in crowded conditions that no one seemed to mind, or even notice.

Just part of sharing whatever was available, big or small, a lot or a little.

> *O Tannenbaum, O Tannenbaum*
>
> *we sang each Christmas Eve*
>
> *at Grandma's house, Columbia, South Dakota*
>
> *in the late thirties, early forties, the fifties*

Generous Spirit

We stuffed fifty-three grandkids
moms and dads, aunts and uncles
into three skinny rooms.

Beyond Surface Manners
Maybe it is a matter of attitude; maybe it is a question of what is really *real;* or then again, maybe it all comes down to doing what feels right, what makes us more, not less. I can only imagine how dreadful a place would be that was reduced to an every-man-for-himself-type formula. Yet are we moving toward that sort of arrangement in urban settings? Places where the clamor to survive grows increasingly intense despite all the gloss and glitter—despite the amazing reservoir of human potential that resides in all the cities of the world.

Oddly enough, we may have forgotten to consider the possible consequences: a world based on elitism, where only the perfect can survive; a world with no capacity for spiritual rejuvenation, meaningful emotion, or hope for the future; one lacking concern for unknown forces that could shield us from our hubris, our blind spots. A world where we have lost our way in pursuit of a hollow victory: a fleeting smugness built on a shaky foundation.

Surely, if we listen to our hearts with a willingness born of love for ourselves and future generations, we would want to take stock of our surroundings from an insightful reference point. And once again, like newborns, we would display a capacity to evaluate what does and doesn't work. Not surprisingly, we might even unravel the puzzle of the millennium: how to achieve true progress as a people without losing sight of our humanity.

But it's my guess that it will take much more than surface manners to accomplish this twenty-first-century feat. Blood, sweat, and tears come to mind, along with the capacity to empathize with the struggles of others, and to possess the ability to make a commitment to rediscovering the power of heart in our daily lives.

As the book *Emotional Intelligence* by Daniel Goleman implies with its intriguing title, we can't be truly smart without the active involvement of our emotional capacities. At the risk of sounding sappy or provincial, nor can we be fully human. A brilliant person (a popular label tossed around so liberally it has lost meaning) without a good heart, without decent instincts for life, can be very dull indeed.

True Blue

A generous spirit can be born from a desire to remain loyal, genuine, and true hearted. "True blue," as people used to say. Or it can spring from a wish, a desire to give others the benefit of the doubt whenever possible, to try and understand or accept people just as they are or as they are attempting to become. Generosity of spirit also shows itself when we acknowledge the shining moments of others: moments when the soul sparkles, emitting a marvelous hue. Being genuinely happy for others when

Generous Spirit

events crystallize for them is a gift of heart like no other. To freely share in someone else's joy is soul-enhancing, an attribute that accents the positive, providing confirmation in the ultimate worth of our journey.

Happy news or happy times are so much *happier* when shared; ideally, with a person who appreciates the personal reasons that make the occasion joyful. Envy, jealousy, and mistrust too often spoil the moment, even between couples in a committed, long-term relationship.

Possessing a generous spirit also allows us to overlook the insignificant slights that are an inevitable part of daily life. Usually on an unintentional basis, but with some frequency, most of us manage to hurt the feelings of those we interact with. Sometimes we realize it, but other times we don't make the connection—unless it's pointed out to us.

The willingness to apologize helps, of course; and when on the receiving end, it also helps to let the little things go by unnoticed. While keeping score is an alternative, many with close ties to the prairie might be inclined to just "let it go."

Not always, but in a place that values constancy, long-term peaceful relations, and yes, friendship, maintaining close ties is an understandable priority.

As we've seen, some prairie residents are apt to loan money and other commodities when they don't have an abundance of either, and though some may find this unwise, imagine the goodwill created, how their generosity enhances their relations with others. Goodwill lacks a price tag—a bonus we draw on indefinitely. When healthy regard exists between people and nations, the world, as a whole, is a better place.

So when the opportunity arises, do something nice for someone; remember how the good feelings linger, past the moment, well into the future and beyond the generous act itself. The key is to believe in the merit of gift offerings, including the gift of self, all year round. (For more about gifts and giving, I strongly recommend the Lewis Hyde classic: *The Gift*.) Possessing a generous spirit means that you, too, *believe:* in magic, in acts of kindness big or small, in yourself and humanity. In an awe-inspiring Universe and its capacity to support your dreams, your travails, your brief journey through a mystical land on an astonishing, make-believe ship called Life.

I was a scrawny, red-headed, freckle-faced tomboy as a young girl. My mother used to express her love by saying, "I love every freckle on your face."

~MARY JEWEL LEDBETTER,
SOUTH DAKOTA RESIDENT, 1920–2012

CHAPTER NINETEEN
Tell Stories

PRESERVING TRADITION, HISTORY, culture, even the more embarrassing moments reflecting the intimate details of our lives offers solace against the unknown—the vastness of space, the inner reaches of the planet we call home, the mysteries of life and death, the amazing parts of ourselves, some good, some bad, that we'll never come to know. Confronted by a wide-open terrain, people who live on the prairie deal with a vast unknown space on an everyday basis, as the prairie itself bespeaks a time and a place that is neither here nor there.

With an otherworldly presence, an aura of the infinite, the grass-covered lands remind us, on a purely visual dimension, of how much we don't know, can never know—not *even* in a lifetime. As an equalizer, as a means for coping with utter insignificance, recording thoughts, events, emotions, and special insights that keep us grounded while simultaneously passing on information to those who follow in our footsteps is of vital importance. For this is the small part we have come to know: the tiny segment of life we have experienced, the gut-wrenching emotions we have lived through, the incredible joys we have known, the people who have crossed our path at the most surprising times, in the most unexpected ways. Unforgettable points of connection (seemingly of the divine, certainly of the magical) when the world, for a brief time at least, makes sense.

Maybe because Dakota's well-known history is so readily apparent—so inherent to the landscape—prairie ways encourage the sharing of stories, formal or informal, embellished or factual, simple or complicated, that convey such moments—the ones we have come to know. In contrast to a vast, uncharted domain, collectively the great unknown, our stories, no matter how detailed, naturally pale in comparison, yet at the same time they offer us respite from an existence of meaningless uncertainty and vagueness.

Getting It Down
One way to tell stories is to record them in a journal or a diary, maybe in a book like this one, maybe in a letter. Think of the wonderful ideas, the eye-opening revelations, and the charming words of romance that have come to life, over the years, on paper. Since the beginning of recorded time, in fact, we've witnessed a seemingly innate need to detail our feelings and perceptions in a way, in a place,

Tell Stories

where we can see the words, read them aloud, capture their true essence, indeed save and share them. In making the words "permanent," by getting them down on paper (or on any substitute), we feel more complete, as though we've managed to extend ourselves into the great unknown, and have effectively etched out a tiny spot in the universe that is concrete and purposeful and ours. Once recorded, sentiments are more real, more alive, and the part of life that seems to slip through our fingers, the part we can't seem to see or capture, is at least momentarily contained.

Is there anything more captivating than a poem that expresses exactly what you want to say? Anything more charming than a handwritten note that brings feelings to light in a way you thought impossible? What about the perfectly inscribed dedication, or the brief personal message attached to a gift of flowers, the unexpected note of thanks? Length doesn't seem to be the issue. Rather, a few carefully chosen words can tell quite a story indeed! (Even those that might be better left untold.) The idea is to care enough to share, in writing, the thoughts and feelings that are too easily overlooked and forgotten.

As noted in an article in *South Dakota Magazine* called "Pages of the Past," when you go back and read your own words—the ones you managed to get down on paper—you come to realize just how much has transpired. This is according to a woman who has been recording her thoughts in diaries since 1931.

Gladys Schaffer, apparently dedicated to recording the days of her life—no secrets, just "weather facts and homestead life"—seems to appreciate the grave importance of little things that when put down on paper take on a fresh quality, a dimension quite unlike the spoken word. *Lake Mitchell opened up for fishing. I didn't go as I had ironing to do. The folks went and they got their limit. Ten apiece.*

An invaluable look at the history of a people, journals provide a glimpse into the soul of the writer, into the collective spirit of a time and a place. Like stars on parade, the kind that travel through the spacious prairie sky so diligently and with such certainty, written entries, each one of them, each word, capture something so fleeting, an ephemeral moment of beauty and distinction that would otherwise be missed forever. For a lifetime of moments are seldom comprised of magnificence, glory, or notoriety; a life, most often, is built on the unspoken value of simple, routine activities that reflect the power of understanding and connectivity with the Universe: with forces seen and unseen.

It's the things we do with frequency, on a regular basis, that carve out our most precise image in the solar system, in the Milky Way galaxy, and needless to say, in our families, neighborhoods, workplaces, and relationships. These taken for granted events, seemingly insignificant, are worth recording.

Sacred Tradition

The Native American heritage puts a considerable amount of emphasis on verbal exchanges: in daily interactions, to record the passage of time, to keep tradition alive. They believe the spoken word is a powerful means of

Tell Stories

communicating ideas, beliefs, an array of possibilities—hopes, dreams, visions of the future—and ancient teachings; *talk, for many,* is at the heart of things. This we've learned from those who have shared the wisdom of the Native American legacy.

In the anthology *Growing Up Native American,* edited and introduced by Patricia Riley, I found this: "The languages and oral traditions of Native American peoples have carried the thoughts and beliefs of their ancestors forward to their descendants in contemporary America. Passed from generation to generation through storytelling, oral traditions represent living libraries containing thousands of years of knowledge and history. . . ." Riley goes on to explain how turbulent times created the eradication of some native languages, but notes that "countless oral traditions still flourish and continue to evolve as new Native American storytellers add their voices to those of their ancestors. . . ."

In *I Tell You Now: Autobiographical Essays by Native American writers,* Simon Ortiz, poet and writer, states: "We come from an ageless, continuing oral tradition that informs us of our values, concepts, and notions as native people . . . despite the brutal efforts of cultural repression that was not long ago outright U.S. policy."

There is a vibrancy about the spoken word, a special quality that encompasses the totality of the individual who is talking or telling a story about the "good old days" (on the prairie, stories like this are alive and well), an inspirational story meant to uplift and motivate, or a childhood nightmare that mysteriously reoccurs. When stories are shared aloud, a sacred sort of harmony can develop between listener and speaker. From intimate settings to gatherings involving hundreds of people, private conversations between couples, whispered tales or secret plans between friends, all in all, the spoken word lends itself to intriguing themes, to poetic connections that sing with a noticeable purity of heart.

Fortunately, many prairie dwellers love to talk, so a good conversation is appreciated, and "talk" is often considered "entertainment" in its own right, no props needed. As a viable way to build bridges between young and old, men and women, poor and rich, races and religions, telling stories on the prairie and elsewhere can help to dissolve barriers, develop rapport and facilitate understanding between diverse, warring groups. Messages and teachings, otherwise resisted, when told in the form of a colorful, captivating story soften emotions and ultimately open doors to personal and spiritual growth.

An interesting thing about a good story is how its most meaningful aspects usually pertain to people of all walks of life. Stories with universal themes are able to supersede differences, perceived and real, by indirectly accentuating the commonalities—between nations, ethnic persuasions, generations, various systems of organized religion. Storytelling, by those who practice it on a professional level or only informally among friends and family, is an art form worth preserving. By helping us keep in touch with our humanity, by nurturing our heartfelt connections, the oral tradition held in such esteem by many Native Americans

Tell Stories

is something to take special note of. A good story has the power to remind us, that, in the end, a life is the sum of mini-stories with a predefined climax and an ending that, while inevitable, is merely one part of a frame around an entire story: a life story. By sharing ourselves through story, we give meaning to our lives.

The Great Mystery

In her novel *Waterlily*, Ella Cara Deloria (a Dakota/Sioux born in 1889 on the Yankton Sioux Reservation in South Dakota), "tells the story of what life was like for a traditional Dakota woman from infancy to early adulthood." A passage from the book (originally published by the University of Nebraska Press), as included in the Riley anthology, clearly illustrates the sentiments, the poignant feelings of a young girl in relation to her mother and vice versa, that when carved out in words are memorable:

> *To Waterlily these were memorable days, for this was the time she began to like her mother best and enjoy being with her more than with the other family members. Before, she had turned as readily to her grandmother, aunts, and other relatives as to her mother—it was the way of related families—but now she was learning to appreciate her mother for the rare and sympathetic person she was. The two were beginning to have little heart-to-heart talks on serious matters that were on Waterlily's mind, which her mother seemed to anticipate.*

There was that lovely afternoon when they went from the camp for a walk, just Blue Bird and her three children, Waterlily, Ohiya, and Smiling One, who was now past two winters. They sat down to rest, and there was nobody and nothing in sight, only country. Blue Bird, looking on her children fondly, said, "Now I am truly happy—surrounded by my children." And this she said because here was one of her rare opportunities to love them without limit, and to show them that she did. In the larger family, where all adults acted parental toward all the children, they tried to be careful not to seem partial to any.

These words, their stirring, timeless message of a shared humanity, are gifts of time, no less. It's possible that I, being a writer, appreciate, and yes, *love,* these words with the sort of passion not shared by the average person, who, with his or her own set of interests doesn't feel the same sense of wonderment or excitement. Yet as I look around me at the world we have created, mostly by accident, but purposefully as well, it becomes apparent that without our stories, indeed, without our histories, collective and individual, we are little more than temporary, frail shadows in a vast and nameless outer space.

Without our stories, do we exist at all?

Each one of us is partially shaped by the words that surround us from day one until our final moment. Messages—positive, negative, confusing, damaging, life preserving—filter into our environment on a nonstop basis, messages composed of words. They are us; we are them. As fundamental to our existence as the air we breathe, words are the building blocks of civilization, of time and place. On the prairie lands I grew up with, words also tell of a time when regrettable events occurred; they tell of invasions, battles, and death.

From Black Elk, a holy man of the Ogalala Lakota/Sioux as told to John G. Neihardt for *Black Elk Speaks:*

> *It was the next summer, when I was 11 years old (1874) that the first sign of trouble came to us. Our band had been camping on Split-Toe Creek in the Black Hills, and from there we moved to Spring Creek, then to Rapid Creek where it comes out into the prairie.*

He goes on to recount numerous moves and meetings, later saying:

> *The nights were sharp now, but the days were clear and still; and while we were camping there I went up into the Hills alone and sat a long while under a tree. I thought maybe my vision would come back and tell me how I could save that country for my people, but I could not see anything clear.*

And finally, he says:

> *Crazy Horse stayed with about a hundred tepees on Powder, and in the middle of the Moon of the Snowblind (March) something bad happened there. It was just daybreak. There was a blizzard and it was very cold. The people were sleeping. Suddenly there*

were many shots and horses galloping through the village. It was the cavalry of the Wasichus, and they were yelling and shooting and riding their horses against the tepees. All the people rushed out and ran, because they were not awake yet and they were frightened.

The attack came in the early morning hours of March 16, 1876, when Colonel Reynolds with "six companies of cavalry attacked Crazy Horse's village."

If we could choose, many of us would wish these words away, pretend these things hadn't occurred. Yet the words confirm the reality, and even when they are painful to acknowledge, it's important that we possess the history, that we have the stories to tell. It's words that give deep meaning to our existence, and in underestimating their power, their purpose, we fail to appreciate their profound significance.

Consider this, an optimistic message from Hiamovi, chief among the Cheyennes and the Dakotas, in his preface to *The Indians' Book: Authentic Native American Legends, Love and Music,* recorded and edited by Natalie Curtis:

There are birds of many colors—red, blue, green, yellow—yet it is all one bird. There are horses of many colors—brown, black, yellow, white—yet it is all one horse. So cattle, so all living things—animals, flowers, trees. So men: in this land where once were only Indians are now men of every color—white, black, yellow, red—yet all one people. That this should

Tell Stories

come to pass was in the heart of the Great Mystery. It is right thus. And everywhere there shall be peace.

Words of beauty, words that convey a depth of understanding and acceptance of the "Great Mystery." And what a magnificent story they tell.

Eternal Spring

Within our stories, within our words, resides an eternal spring, in that inside each of us lies the unlimited power to craft a better tomorrow, one that more clearly expresses our deepest desires and secret yearnings, our dreams, visions, and hopes. One that outlines the kind of world we want to live in, that defines the world we so desperately want to leave behind for those who will follow us, ever so willingly, ever so fearfully or bravely.

By keeping our stories alive and circulating, we preserve a sense of community, and in many ways we help prepare future generations for the inevitable challenges that lie ahead. They can learn from our mistakes; take heart in our undaunted courage; hold the wisdom of past ways close, like a protective shield against the onslaught of time, the onrush of fads, fantasy, and folly. For surely the settlers of the 1800s, the Native Americans of the great plains, would hope we've all learned something from the past, the past our stories have captured and won't let us forget or erase.

In honoring their memory, let us always value their struggle to understand and to survive a changing world that seemed to be taking them down a very rocky path indeed. We cannot change the past, but the past *can* change us, and within that sentiment is additional cause, justifiable reason, to believe in an eternal spring.

Ojibway elder and storyteller, Ignatia Broker, in sharing her story about her great-great-grandmother, passes on wisdom and hope to a young girl in preparation for a move made necessary "because there is another people who are fast coming. . . ."

> *Mother looked down at her fragile daughter, she who was much smaller than the other children of her age. She brushed Oona's black shining hair and lifted up the small oval face with the huge dark eyes.*
>
> *"It is sad to be leaving, my Oona," said Mother, "but in one's life there are many times when one must leave a place of happiness for the unknown. I have done this many times, but the beauty of a life remains forever in the heart. You must remember the beauty that was here. Go, my daughter, and say the words of friendship to those who were your playmates."*

None of this is meant to suggest that we should get lost in our stories, never seeing the present moment. But in fully acknowledging our stories, perhaps, we can see the present moment even better.

That it will never come again is what makes life sweet.
~EMILY DICKINSON
1830–1886

CHAPTER TWENTY
Come and Go

Now, AS WE TAKE ONE FINAL LOOK, hopefully a lasting one, at the prairie that is so very dear to my heart, at the lands that have been such a marvelous teacher, such a treasured friend, it's appropriate to consider the majestic blue skies and the sometimes daunting landscape from a broader perspective. How does this well of prairie knowledge best fit into the limited number of years each of us has the privilege of living, into a life span that rarely exceeds 100 years in comparison with the virtual agelessness of the prairies?

Doubtless to say, you may discover this book as a young person, a retired person, maybe as someone who plans to live forever—if only we could make it so.

What can you derive from this book of prairie wisdom, regardless of your age, challenges, hopes and dreams, besides the ideas already revealed?

Always Returning

Initially, that nothing in life is wildly permanent.

Even now, as I tell you about the marvels of the prairie, about its charms, development plans threaten to encroach on the natural beauty of the native prairie; we cannot assume it will be with us indefinitely. "Progress" does take its toll—on all of us, on all parts of the globe. And so it is that in our efforts to make everything, including the prairie, conform to our endless demands and ongoing needs as a civilization, to our wishes, we may witness its eventual demise. Of course, there are many who scoff at the idea: Who would bother developing *that* part of the country when clearly it lacks contemporary appeal?

But, almost inevitably, there comes a time when things do change, for better or worse, and though it may be impossible to envision at this point in our history, we know from experience that it happens, sometimes with tremendous surprise, agitation, and strife. One day it's entirely possible that we will wake up to find the prairie lands altered, made into something "more useful" or "more profitable."

To that end, there is tremendous merit in taking the time to view these lands with an eye for its distinct qualities—the ones that offer a unique perspective on the mysteries and magic of life.

The Morning Light

First and foremost, we have learned that the prairie—the place, the culture, and the people—doesn't represent a nirvana; quite often the prairie's everlasting beauty is best found in the eye of the beholder. So it is that the morning light can indeed play tricks on those who wake up to the land of penetrating light and sky. There are mornings when the scene generates an expansive, peaceful, wide-open feeling—secure, warm, and inviting. Other times, the vast, untamed area may feel empty and barren, nearly overpowering in its magnitude, its starkness. And sometimes the waving grasses, the intense sky, seem to silently mock all of mankind.

Captured within this landscape is a poetic mix of extremes. Like "The Velocity of Love," a piano piece by Suzanne Ciani, gazing at the prairie, living in its midst, can evoke feelings of quiet despair, enraptured bliss, discontentment, and sudden restlessness—all at the same precise moment. The primary differential is what *you* bring to it: the morning light through which you view the immense space, vast distances, and the quality of sameness. An excellent barometer of your internal state, one difficult to deny, prairie spaces, indeed, prairie places, don't encourage escape from what is. Like a wise and knowing teacher, the landscape seems to insist that each person find his or her way—there when needed but definitely not offering a utopian existence or a place to shrink from the inevitable challenges of life.

The prairie won't insulate you from yourself.

Rather, it will magnify your strengths and weaknesses, your silly side, your serious side, and the middle ground where you simply try to be yourself—discovering who you are and what you are all about, forcing you to contend with the raw material you brought into the world, whatever that may be. On a paradoxical level, however, the prairie offers us comfort and solace against a harsh, often uncaring world—the one we all must take responsibility for creating. Yet this is appropriate.

It has been said many times that life is paradoxical, and no matter how ill-equipped we feel to navigate our way through this sort of maze, we have little choice. Certainly not if we are committed to self-discovery, something that requires consistent ingenuity and a capacity to confront ourselves on a primitive level. We know personal truths can be sobering, if not unnerving and difficult to accept.

But the people or places that offer us the rare gift of self-knowledge are treasures. In their presence, it's possible to feel their heartfelt concern, to sense their belief in the encouraging reservoir of human potential residing within each person. As such, these sorts of influences, people or places or events, have a tendency to draw something—talents, abilities, feelings—from us that we scarcely knew existed. These are people who detect the truths we are unable to see ourselves; and by pushing our buttons, getting us all riled up, believing in us for no good or apparent reason—offering no room for excuses—we grow. While we may find the process uncomfortable and annoying, even painful, because of these circumstances genuine caring can be experienced.

No matter how you view the prairies, no matter how you experience them—as a visitor, an inhabitant, or as a reader of this book—try to remember the gifts, the charms of the heart, readily offered by a people and a place that is barren yet bountiful; isolated and remote yet incredibly endearing; peaceful and freeing yet confining; poor yet rich. For this is a place that rarely allows people to settle for less than they are capable of being and becoming, and that, to me, is the greatest gift of all.

Nothing comes easy in an area some love to ridicule. A place where the economy is often stagnant, where history announces the capacity for failure, where few secrets are kept; a place many must *learn to love*. Clearly, this is a place where nature is *the* force to reckon with, where people are reminded daily of their comparative insignificance, and it's a place where evidence of a higher power is so vast, so clear, as to be somewhat intimidating. And perplexing. And humility-provoking.

A forty-seven-year resident of the area, the editor and publisher of *South Dakota Magazine,* Bernie Hunhoff, shared this when responding to interview questions: "Anyone who can understand and appreciate the wonder of nature and yet deny a Higher Power is a champion of cynicism." His astute observation is a sharp reminder of the general ease with which some have allowed a disbelief in nearly everything previously held sacred and true to go by the wayside.

Religion is largely a personal preference.

But the capacity to believe in something or someone other than what can be seen and witnessed firsthand is necessary to our survival as a species. Without a capacity to believe—in ourselves, in others, in unseen powers, in the basic goodness of womankind, mankind—our ship is sinking fast.

As the morning light eases its way into your bedroom, consider anew your internal state: How does it read, what does it tell you about yourself? What is the state of *your* soul; do *you* care?

Glad Tidings

As testament to my belief in humanity—as an ordinary and humble spokesperson for a place that taught me a good deal about myself, and about life—I suggest the most painful lessons are these: *Your life's journey is not a predictable one; if you allow yourself room to grow, if you have the courage to grow when the opportunity presents itself, the vast web of life will take you places you never dreamt of, rattle you in ways you thought impossible, move you to quiet despair and complete confusion, point you in inexplicable directions that cause you to question everything, push you to change your thinking, to alter your beliefs and assumptions, to admit defeat, to start over time and time again. And to know, truly know from direct experience, that no one is immune from the hardships of life—its ups and downs, puzzling manifestations, and unbearable sorrows—because mortality and suffering are the nature of things at this point in human evolution. If you care deeply about anyone or anything, eventually, you will have to part company in a planned sort of way, or otherwise.*

So it's quite possible the day will come when you will be required to leave your current, possibly happy, surroundings in a quest for greater knowledge, challenge, love, or purpose of heart. As many have learned, to believe otherwise, to think, with false assurance, that you are immune from the normal pressures and learning experiences of human existence is to court disaster, to ensure a disruption of immense proportion.

Like the massive earthquake that wasn't predicted, the blizzard that wasn't supposed to materialize, the drought that shouldn't have occurred, the flood that wasn't anticipated, the prairie fire that should never have started, nature reminds us—if we will only listen—that we are not the ultimate powers in the Universe. Important, worthy of love and second chances, of course; capable of growth and change, of making mistakes yet learning and surviving, absolutely; none of which, however, makes us invincible or omnipotent—it only makes us human. And there is a big difference.

But wondrously, therein I detect an element of optimism: a reason to feel hopeful about the future. Not designed as perfect creatures, nor intended to experience predictably safe or easy lives, we possess a built-in assurance for "success" on a spiritual, metaphysical level. And while this means accepting the temporary nature of life, as we know it, and perceiving the need to "come and go" during the defining moments of our lives, we can, with courage and assurance, peer into the window of our hearts once again to access a road map already drawn and marked, patiently waiting for our return.

We know the way back to our hearts.

We've only lost sight of the path, a condition we can still remedy, even now, at this point in history. Maybe it's

Always Returning

a matter of letting more light into our lives, of trusting our intuition—listening to it once again—of refusing to simply overlook intolerable conditions—being true to ourselves—and of knowing when to stay, when to leave: the task of a lifetime.

One key is to never say never.

Stay open to surprise; anticipate change and challenge; be willing to listen to your heart once more—to *care*. Most of all, give your soul room to breathe.

In searching for the place of wisdom that lies within, that place where your heart resides, it helps to view all places and stations in life as temporary stopping points where something of value can be learned; that way, you will know when it is time to go. For nothing subdues the spirit more than to live a life that is without heart, without a purpose that is joyful—that adds meaning to your existence. By holding on to a path that has lost this quality—by not knowing when it's time to go—you can greatly limit the power of heart in your life, letting your deep cynicism spill over into the lives of those around you. Ultimately, the choice is yours, but in the end, the effect is truly global.

And if a deep wound should present itself, suddenly and with a mighty force, remember life—no matter where you live or what you do—is a precarious balance between the known and the unknown, the expected and the unexpected. So even though we all must "come and go" in a very literal sense, an inevitable consequence of our mortality, it's what we do with the time we have that counts. If we are in touch with our hearts, with our spirituality, if we are true to our beliefs, a certain measure of immortality is bound to be ours.

As evidenced by the lives we touch in a memorable and positive fashion, the love we give and leave behind is indeed . . . timeless.

EPILOGUE

Just as there may be a time to leave a place—the prairie, for instance—and continue a life's journey elsewhere, this is an opportune time for our nation, indeed, for our world, to consider its direction. Is it time to change course, to rethink our focus, evaluate priorities—or consider anew the heart of our nation, and our world?

Clearly, many of our most pressing questions will continue to go unanswered, even as we try, hope, and plan our way into the next century. But one thing is certain—in a place where life is reduced to the basics, where many of life's modern-day complexities fade, where one can pull back the curtain of time to reveal natural, human elements, we're still granted clues about our survival as a civilization. So if there is one thing the prairie offers us now, it's yet another chance to find our way back to our hearts: a place we know but perhaps abandoned in exchange for something called progress.

Yet if we no longer truly listen to our hearts, how can we begin to know which is what? What appears to be progress may be ten steps backward, or much worse.

Always Returning

For this anniversary edition in 2014, the impact of global warming comes to mind with the recent report from NASA about the inevitable collapse of the West Antarctic ice sheet. New challenges are upon us in so many guises, and we need creative solutions, yes, but we also need a deeper awareness to guide us. Our internal compass must be faithfully consulted if we are to motivate ourselves and others. Possessing knowledge isn't the same as looking deeply (and willingly) at a situation for the root cause that may have more to do with human nature than anything else. In this vast, interconnected world, viable answers must be created and imagined for different levels of reality, some of them buried within the many layers of truth that coexist on a home we all call Earth.

Perhaps this is a test of life and death magnitude. Can we all come together in an effort to survive, to access the deeper answers that only can be found within?

Again, we are pioneers faced with a daunting new landscape; again, we are contending with forces well beyond our control or complete understanding. I wonder how we will do.

REFERENCES

American Renaissance Chautauqua Companion Reader, presented by the Great Plains Chautauqua Society, Inc.

Beck, Charlotte Joko. *Now Zen.* San Francisco: HarperSan Francisco, 1995.

Brandt, Charles. *Meditations from the Wilderness.* Toronto: HarperCollins Publishers Ltd., 1997.

Broker, Ignatica. *Night Flying Woman: An Ojibway Narrative.* St. Paul, MN: Minnesota Historical Society, 1983.

Chaffee, John. *The Thinker's Way.* Boston: Little, Brown and Company, 1998.

Curtis, Natalie, ed. *The Indians' Book.* New York: Gramercy Books, 1994.

Deloria, Ella Cara. *Waterlily.* Lincoln, NE: University of Nebraska Press, 1988.

Fanebust, Wayne. *Tales of Dakota Territory.* Sioux Falls: Mariah, 1994.

Hasselstrom, Linda, Gaydell Collier, and Nancy Curtis, eds. *Leaning into the Wind.* Boston and New York: Houghton-Mifflin (Marc Jaffe), 1997.

Heat-Moon, William Least. *PrairyErth.* Boston: Houghton-Mifflin (Peter Davison), 1991.

Herseth, Lorna Buntrock. *Autobiography.* Northfield: Fairway Foods, 1994.

Hopcke, Robert H. *There Are No Accidents.* New York: Riverhead Books, 1997.

Madson, John. *Where the Sky Began.* Ames: Iowa State University Press, 1996. First edition, New York: Houghton-Mifflin, 1982.

Moore, Thomas. *Care of the Soul.* New York: HarperCollins, 1992.

Neihardt, John G. *Black Elk Speaks.* Reprinted by permission of the University of Nebraska Press. Copyright © 1932, 1959, 1972, by John G. Neihardt. Copyright © 1961 by the John G. Neihardt Trust.

Norris, Kathleen. *Dakota.* Boston and New York: Houghton-Mifflin, 1993.

Riley, Patricia, ed. *Growing up Native American.* New York: William Morrow & Company (Bill Adler), 1993.

Rölvaag, O.E. *Giants in the Earth.* New York: Harper & Row Perennial Library, 1927.

Schuler, Harold H. *Pierre Since 1910.* Freeman, SD: Pine Hill Press, Inc. 1998.

Swann, Brian and Arnold Krupat, eds. *I Tell You Now: Autobiographical Essays by Native American Writers.* Lincoln, NE: University of Nebraska Press, 1987.

Wee, Karen H. *The Book of Hearts.* Goodhue, MN: The Black Hat Press, 1993.

Wyman, Walker D, recorded by, from the original notes of Bruce Siberts. *Nothing but Prairie and Sky.* Norman and London: University of Oklahoma Press, 1954.

PERIODICALS

Adams, Robert. "Dakota Skies," *South Dakota Magazine,* March/April, 1996.

Lange, Cindy. "Pages of the Past," *South Dakota Magazine,* May/June, 1996.

Peterson, Mark. "Wide Open Space," *South Dakota Magazine,* January/February, 1996.

ABOUT THE AUTHOR

D.A. (DAISY) HICKMAN is a poet, an author, and the 2010 founder of **SunnyRoomStudio**—a creative, sunny space for kindred spirits. Hickman holds a master's degree in sociology from Iowa State University, and earned her bachelor's degree at Stephens College in Columbia, Missouri. A member of the Academy of American Poets and the South Dakota State Poetry Society, Hickman is at work on her first poetry collection and on a memoir.

The first edition of this book was published in 1999 by William Morrow (Eagle Brook imprint) as *Where the Heart Resides: Timeless Wisdom of the American Prairie*.

For author updates or to subscribe to Hickman's blog, visit SunnyRoomStudio.com or follow her on Facebook and Twitter. You may send relevant email to wisdom@sunnyroomstudio.com.